# Bridge for Beginners

The authors of this authoritative and lucid volume are players and bridge writers of international repute; and these twelve concise lessons have for some years served as the basis for tuition at the London School of Bridge.

The book contains simple charts and many other aids to help the beginner learn quickly and enjoy the most fascinating and popular of indoor games.

'Should prove a veritable godsend'
**Country Life**

'Most capably done'
**British Bridge World**

'Excellent'
**Times Literary Supplement**

**Also available in Pan**

# BRIDGE
# FOR BEGINNERS

**Victor Mollo** and **Nico Gardener**

Pan Books  London and Sydney

First published 1956 by Gerald Duckworth & Co Ltd
First Pan Edition published 1963
This revised edition published 1986 by Pan Books Ltd,
Cavaye Place, London SW10 9PG
9 8 7 6 5 4 3 2 1
©Victor Mollo and Nico Gardener 1958
ISBN 0 330 29611 6
Photoset by Parker Typesetting Service, Leicester
Printed and bound in Great Britain by
Richard Clay (The Chaucer Press) Ltd, Bungay, Suffolk

# CONTENTS

## *Part Three*

# PREFACE

Many contract bridge books have been written for beginners –
for those who have already begun to play. This one is designed
primarily for those who have not.

That almost anyone can master and enjoy the game is proved
by the fact that there are today over 3 million players in the
United Kingdom. For the United States the official figure is 25
million, which shows that on both sides of the Atlantic more
grown-ups play bridge than any other game, indoors or out.

Football, cricket, boxing, all the sports which make the
headlines, command huge audiences. Two men are in the ring,
twenty-two players run up and down a field, and tens of
thousands watch them doing it. In bridge, all the numbers are
made up, not of spectators, but of active participants. Men and
women, young and old, weak and strong, all can and do play
star parts.

No equipment is needed beyond a table and a pack of cards.
The hour of day does not matter. For one of the charms of
bridge is that it can be played by anyone, at any time, in any
place, and the English climate itself can do nothing to mar its
joys. What is more, unlike other forms of entertainment, it
costs nothing.

The marvel is not that so many millions play bridge already,
but that so many others do not. They miss a lot in life, and for
no good reason.

For many people the chief deterrent to taking up the game is
the first step – getting a start. A novice hesitates to inflict
himself on his more experienced friends at the bridge table. Yet
how can he gain experience without first being a novice?

The purpose of this book is to break the vicious circle – to take the beginner through his novitiate, eliminating the tedium and the labours. There is nothing experimental about the methods. The lessons, and the exercises which follow them, have been tried and tested over a period of years by the London School of Bridge. Thousands of beginners have learned the game this way, and can now look forward to enjoying its pleasures for many years to come. In bridge, as in all games, you will need practice, but after reading these pages you will have no need to fear it, for you will know enough not to spoil the game for others.

Before the curtain goes up, take a word of advice from the authors. If anything puzzles you – it may be the scoring – leave it aside and read on. When you come back to it later, the mist will have cleared.

Mark Twain found it easy to give up smoking, for he had done it thousands of times. You will find it easier still to acquire the bridge habit. Millions all over the world have done it already, and rare indeed is the player with the urge to give it up.

# EXPLANATION OF EXERCISES

The purpose of the exercises which follow every lesson is to allow the reader to practise as he learns. The beginner should not be disappointed if he fails to find the correct answers. He is expected to make mistakes – in plenty. He will learn much from them, and more still, when he comes back, later, to the questions which defied him at the first attempt.

In bridge, as in other fields, success is born of confidence – the knowledge that everyday situations have been met and mastered. That means experience. And it is to provide the reader with experience that he is invited to test his technique – step by step, as he acquires it – on some 200 questions, which cover every phase of the game. If he can register a score of 60 per cent or better, he need have no inhibitions about joining his friends at the card table. It may well be, in fact, that he will know more about bridge than they do. With a little practice added to the theory, he will soon gain the confidence which is the key to success.

Detailed answers to the exercises will be found on pages 168–192.

## Part One

### LESSON I

# BRIDGE EXPLAINED: THEORY

**What is the Game?** Fashions in card games come and go. But bridge remains forever popular and forever in season. Derived from whist – which is to cards what the coelecanth is to fish – bridge is *the* game for four players. Its essential feature is that it is a partnership – or rather, two partnerships – like doubles at tennis.

The partners face each other and their interests are identical.

**Trumps.** Unlike whist, the trumps at bridge are not announced before the deal. The two sides compete for the right to make their own trumps – or no-trumps* – and the highest bidder wins. This is known as the

**Auction.** It starts with the dealer and proceeds clockwise round the table. Each player, in turn, bids his values – or lack of values. Normally, though not always, the stronger side wins the auction and plays the hand.

**Declarer.** Once the auction is over, the spot-light turns on declarer. Even if the last bid was made by his partner, declarer is always the player who *first* called the denomination – the particular suit or no-trumps – in which the hand is played. He

---

* In no-trump contracts all suits are equal and the highest card of the suit led, by either side, wins the trick.

is in charge of the contract – the final bid. Declarer plays the cards for his side and has all the fun while it lasts. His partner becomes–

**Dummy,** and exposes his thirteen cards on the table, opposite declarer, so that all can see them. Dummy can draw attention to irregularities, but must otherwise remain taciturn and inscrutable.

**Defenders.** Proceedings for the defence are always opened by the player on declarer's left, and his first card is known as the opening lead. Thereafter, each side tries to do down the other. Declarer strives to fulfil his contract – to gather the number of tricks announced in the final bid. Defenders seek to break or set him.

**Tricks.** Each player, in turn, follows to every lead and the four cards constitute a trick. This falls to the side which has played the highest card of the suit led. As in Whist, a player is obliged to follow suit if he can. If he has no more cards left in that suit, he can ruff – win the trick with a trump.

**Game and Rubber.** The objective at bridge is the rubber. It corresponds to a frame at snooker or a set at tennis. After the rubber, existing partnerships dissolve and the players go home – or more likely, start another. To win the rubber, a partnership must make *two* games. And that brings us face to face with the scoresheet.

**Scoring.** Don't be despondent. Admittedly, scoring is dull and dreary – like doing up one's shoelaces. But it is just as necessary and calls for no more skill. As you will see from the illustration on page 15, the score sheet is divided into parallel columns, headed by the tell-tale words 'We' and 'They' – our score and theirs. A line is drawn across the page, traversing those columns horizontally. Keep your eye on that horizontal line.

Everything that is achieved on the way to game and rubber is scored *below* the line. Everything else is recorded above.

**Points for Game.** To make game – half the rubber – the side that plays the hand needs 100 points below the line. This can be done in one fell swoop – by *bidding and making* game on a single hand; or in stages – through two or more *part scores*, which, between them, add up to 100.

That vital 100 is measured in three different currencies. The hardest is no-trumps; then the majors – spades and hearts; and lastly the minors – diamonds and clubs.

For the total to come to 100 on a single hand, the side that plays it must *bid and make: nine tricks in no-trumps; ten tricks in the major suits or eleven in the minor suits.*

## Tricks for Game

| | | One trick | Two tricks | Three tricks | Four tricks | Five tricks | Six tricks | Seven tricks |
|---|---|---|---|---|---|---|---|---|
| | No trumps | 40 | 70 | 100 | 130 | 160 | 190 | 220 |
| Major suits | Spades | 30 | 60 | 90 | 120 | 150 | 180 | 210 |
| | Hearts | 30 | 60 | 90 | 120 | 150 | 180 | 210 |
| Minor suits | Diamonds | 20 | 40 | 60 | 80 | 100 | 120 | 140 |
| | Clubs | 20 | 40 | 60 | 80 | 100 | 120 | 140 |

GAME IS 100 OR OVER

At first sight, it may seem odd that it should need ten tricks in spades, at 30 apiece, to carry the total past the 100 mark. Many a mathematician would make the total 300. And his estimate for eleven tricks in diamonds would be 220. Which only shows that mathematicians don't know everything.

In bridge, the bidding and scoring start with the *seventh* trick. The first six are taken for granted. It needs *seven* tricks (6 plus 1) to make one, and there is no such thing as a bid of less than one. To call three hearts means to contract for *nine* tricks with hearts as trumps. A grand slam, in which declarer needs all thirteen tricks, is a contract of seven (6 plus 7 equals 13).

This, of course, is reproduced on the score-sheet. Four diamonds means ten tricks (4 plus 6), but it is worth 80 only – four times 20. So it needs *five* diamonds for game.

Observe that no-trumps enjoy a curious privilege. The *first* trick (that means the seventh, of course) counts as 40. Thereafter, no trumps have the same value as spades and hearts. But the odd 10 points make a difference. Only three no-trumps (40 plus 30 plus 30 equals 100) are needed for game. In spades or hearts one more trick is wanted to top the century.

**Vulnerability.** As soon as one side gets game, it becomes what is known as vulnerable. Opponents lose any *part score* they may have made towards their own game – or rubber – and must start afresh towards the 100 mark. The part score points, as all points scored during the play, count in the final reckoning, when accounts for the rubber are made up.

Having made game, it is usual to draw a line, below the figures, and to extend it across both columns, We and They.

The diagram opposite shows that the other side made 40 – one no-trump or two in one of the minors – on the first deal. Then We made 120 and killed their partial score. Had They made 40 *after* our game, no line would be drawn across their column and they would still have a part score towards game.

| We | They |
|---|---|
|  |  |
| 120 | 40 |
|  |  |

**Score Above the Line.** Only the progress made towards game and rubber is put down below the line. It is a record of the contracts that are actually *made*.

What, then, goes above? The answer is:

1. Overtricks.
2. Undertricks.
3. Penalties.
4. Slam Bonuses.
5. Honours.

Let us take them one by one:

**Overtricks.** Since declarer's side can only take credit below the line for the tricks it undertakes to make – i.e. the contract – extra tricks, if any, are inscribed above. They swell the total without helping towards game.

The contract is three hearts and declarer makes ten tricks – one over. His side puts down 90 (part score) below the line and 30 above – for the overtrick.

**Undertricks.** Often enough, the contract is broken. Declarer *goes down*. That is the current expression, and it is usual to say, *one* down or *two* down – according to the number of tricks by which declarer falls short of the contract.

This time, They do the scoring. If declarer's side is not vulnerable, going down costs 50 a trick. Vulnerable, the rate is 100.

**Penalties.** A penalty is an undertrick, only more so.

When one side believes that the other has overbid – has contracted for more tricks than it can win – either defender can double. That has the same effect as raising the stakes; not just doubling the stakes, mark you, for the difference is often greater.

For the *first* trick – one down – the double means exactly what it says. Non-vulnerable, declarer's side pays 100 instead of 50. Vulnerable, the price is 200 in place of 100. Then the rates go up by *200* for every further undertrick non-vulnerable, and by *300* vulnerable.

Going down, particularly when opponents double, can be expensive, and that is why the score above the line may well exceed the bonus for winning the rubber.

|  | Non-vulnerable | | Vulnerable | |
|---|---|---|---|---|
|  | Undoubled | Doubled | Undoubled | Doubled |
| 1 down | 50 | 100 | 100 | 200 |
| 2 down | 100 | 300 | 200 | 500 |
| 3 down | 150 | 500 | 300 | 800 |
| 4 down | 200 | 700 | 400 | 1,100 |
| 5 down | 250 | 900 | 500 | 1,400 |
| 6 down | 300 | 1,100 | 600 | 1,700 |

The above table explains better than any dictionary the origin of the word 'vulnerable'. It implies that, after scoring a game, going down becomes a costly business. Therefore, the side that is vulnerable has to take extra care.

**Making Doubled Contract.** Sometimes, of course, the defenders misjudge – or misdefend – the hand, and a doubled contract is made. Then the figures below the line are doubled and declarer also takes 50 points above the line for the 'insult'. If he makes overtricks, he collects 100 a time if he is not vulnerable, and 200, if he is vulnerable. It is a flat rate all the way.

Whatever the result, no hand can yield more than one game. The surplus over and above the 100 mark cannot be carried on towards the next game. But there is such a thing as being doubled into game, for if the contract is made, the figures below the line are also doubled.

The contract, let us say, is three diamonds (nine tricks). That comes to 60. If opponents double, and declarer succeeds in making his contract, the total is 120, which is more than enough for game. The bonus for the 'insult' (50 points) does not come into it, for it is entered above the line.

**Redouble.** Occasionally, an irresistible defender meets an immovable declarer, and the double is followed by a redouble. This time, even a mathematician can work it out. All that need be done is to multiply by two the doubled score. Whatever the figures would have been if the contract had been doubled, the redouble makes them twice as large. Only the 'insult' remains unchanged at 50 – if declarer makes his contract.

Just as a double indicates confidence on the part of the defence that the contract will be broken, so a redouble reflects confidence on the part of declarer or his partner that it will be made.

**Slam Bonus.** For calling and making slams there is a bonus which varies according to vulnerability. To get the bonus for a small slam, declarer's side must bid and make twelve tricks, and for a grand slam, all thirteen tricks.

The bonus is 500 for a small slam, and 1,000 for a grand slam, non-vulnerable; and 750 and 1,500 respectively, when declarer's side is vulnerable.

Doubles and redoubles do not affect the slam bonus. But a slam always means a game, as well, for the score below the line can never be less than 120 – six diamonds or six clubs.

**Honours.** This is an archaic feature of the scoring and has been discarded in match play, though it still applies to rubber bridge.

When a player holds the four aces in his own hand or in dummy at a no-trump contract, or all five trump honours (A, K, Q, J, 10) in a suit bid, his side takes 150 points above the line. Four of the five top honours in trumps earn a bonus of 100. Three aces in the same hand earn no increment.

**Rubber Points.** The first side to make two games wins the rubber. If the other side has a game, the winners take 500. If it is a 'love' rubber, the bonus is 700.

When bridge is played for money, the losers pay on the difference in the total scores. All the figures – above the line and below – are added up. It is the practice to name the stakes per 100 points, and to ignore the balance, unless it exceeds 50. That way, 750 is only 7 points, but 760 becomes 8.

Now the worst is nearly over. We have acquired a smattering of the terminology, and, better still, we know how to score.

In the next lesson we shall go through the movements and noises round the table.

### Exercises

1. You bid two hearts and make nine tricks.

   (a) What do you put down below the line?
   (b) What do you put above the line?

(c) If you now bid and make one spade, will that give you game?

2. At game all, opponents bid four spades and win nine tricks.

(a) Do you score the result in their column or in yours?
(b) Do you score the result above or below the line?

3. On the first deal you bid and make three no-trumps. On the next deal you call three hearts, which opponents double. What is the score, and where do you record it, if you make:

(a) Seven tricks.
(b) Nine tricks.
(c) Ten tricks.

4. On the first deal of the rubber you bid and make six diamonds.

(a) What do you put down below and above the line?
(b) What is the answer to (a) if opponents doubled?
(c) If they doubled and you redoubled?

5. You call three diamonds and make ten tricks. Your partner's diamonds were the A K Q and you had J 10.

(a) What do you score below the line?
(b) What do you score above the line?

6. At love all, opponents play the hand in three hearts, which you double. They make eight tricks. Your trump holding was: A Q J 10.

(a) What do you score below the line?
(b) What do you score above the line?

7. On the first hand of the rubber opponents bid and make four hearts. Then you make two clubs. On the third deal they call two spades and make seven tricks.

(a) What is the balance of points at this stage of the rubber?
(b) If, on the fourth deal, you bid and make a grand slam, will the rubber be over?

8. Your contract, at love all, is one no-trump redoubled. What do you score, below and above the line, if you make:

(a) Seven tricks.
(b) Eight tricks.
(c) Ten tricks.

9. The player on your left calls four hearts. All pass. Whose turn is it to lead?

10. The player on your right deals and bids one club. His partner responds three no-trumps and all pass. Whose turn is it to lead?

11. Your side only is vulnerable. Opponents bid four spades, which your partner doubles. Your side makes five tricks. What is the score on this deal?

## LESSON II

# BRIDGE EXPLAINED: PRACTICE

**Going Through the Movements.** Everything must have a beginning. At bridge it is the moment when the four players cut for partners.

**The Cut.** The player who cuts the highest card partners the one with the second highest. And he has all the initial privileges. It is for him to choose the seats and the cards, and to deal – one card at a time – starting with the player on his left. As at whist, every player is dealt thirteen cards – a quarter of the pack. While the deal is in progress, dealer's partner shuffles the other pack – for it is usual to play with two packs.

Having shuffled, he places the pack on his right, ready for the next deal.

**First to Speak.** The dealer is always the first to speak – to make the first bid in the auction. With a poor hand, he *passes* – which is the verb for saying 'No bid'. And if all four players pass, the hand is thrown in, and the cards are dealt by the next man. Since all the movements are clockwise, the cards are always dealt by the player on the left of the previous dealer.

**Opening the Bidding.** The cards are not thrown in very often – perhaps once in, say, twenty or thirty deals. Usually, one of the players has enough strength to say something. Though there is no way of contracting for less than seven (one) tricks, subject to that, the opener can call as much or as little as he likes. Nine times out of ten, at least, the opening is one of something. Then the auction develops, reflecting the balance of strength between the two sides. Every player in turn can call, but it must be something *higher* than the call before – either more tricks or the same number of tricks in a higher denomination.

**Ranking of the Suits.** As we saw in the first lesson no-trumps have absolute priority, being worth more than any of the four suits. Then come spades, hearts, diamonds and clubs, in that order.

Spades and hearts are known as the majors, diamonds and clubs as the minors. But spades rank higher than hearts, though they count the same in the scoring. And diamonds rank higher than clubs.

If the opening bid is one heart, the next caller can bid one spade – because spades rank higher than hearts. But in the minors – diamonds or clubs – he would have to bid two. Over no-trumps, of course, no suit can be bid at the same level, for none ranks as high.

A pass is always in order, and a player can double any bid made by his opponents. There is no such thing as doubling a bid made by partner. Neither can a player double his opponents after partner has already doubled the *same bid*.

**Auction Closes.** Sometimes only one side takes part in the bidding. At other times there is keen competition for the right to play the hand. The auction is brought to a close by *three* successive passes. This means that every player can intervene after every bid made by another player.

A double or redouble is a bid and keeps the auction alive for the next three players.

**Contract.** The final bid – which precedes three 'no bids' – settles the contract, and thereby decides the number of tricks to be made, and the denomination in which the hand is played.

**Ethics.** *What* a player should bid will be discussed in the next lesson. *How* he should bid can be laid down firmly this minute. The manner must be impersonal and the voice even. That is all. But it is important to cultivate the right habits from the beginning. Players of experience, who ought to know better, are sometimes apt to betray elation at the sight of a picture gallery, or dejection when they are confronted by a collection of 'tram-tickets'. Intonation and inflection, and even bouncing up and down in one's chair, all are frowned upon in the best circles. The word for these emotional aids to science is 'unethical' and that is almost a synonym for cheating.

**Play Begins.** As soon as the opening lead touches the table, dummy's hand goes down, and declarer pauses. That is the moment for a short huddle – to plan and work things out.

The novice is tempted to play quickly to the first few tricks, when there are plenty of high cards around. Then, as aces and kings get fewer, he slows down and regrets his early impetuosity.

Try to sketch a plan of campaign *before* playing to the first trick. Count the certain winners – the top trumps, the aces, the tricks they can't take away from you. And count your losers – the tricks you can't take away from them. You may not find it too easy until you gain experience, if only because so many tricks are uncertain either way. Try to plan ahead all the same, even if you do not get beyond the first few moves.

As with rackets and golf clubs, so with cards, there is a right way and a wrong way to handle them. And learning the correct approach from the start shapes the future.

**Taking Tricks.** The pause is now over and declarer can play to the first trick from the 'table'. This is dummy, and dummy always goes first; then the second defender, and, finally, declarer himself. There is nothing to remember here, for all the movements in bridge follow the same course – to the left (clockwise). But it is important to note *which hand* takes the trick. The lead to every trick is made by the hand which wins the one before. And that makes all the difference to the play.

**Playing Out of Turn.** No one should play out of turn – before the hand on the right. There are penalties for all infringements of the rules, and some of them are severe. Don't worry about them at this stage. Just take it back – the card or the bid – and smile sweetly all round the table.

**Gathering the Tricks.** Declarer stacks his tricks neatly in front of him. And *one* of the defenders does the same for his side. All this tidiness is not just a homage to the laws of symmetry or a protest against the Bohemian way of life. The idea is that every player should always know the situation – how many cards have gone, and how many tricks have been won and lost. Also, it may be necessary, after the hand is over, to look up a trick in case of a revoke.

**The Revoke.** A player is under obligation to follow suit, if he can do so. Should he 'show out' when he can follow, he will be guilty of a revoke. For this, the penalty is to transfer two tricks from the offenders to their opponents – one only if the trick on which the revoke occurred was won by the non-offending side.

To revoke intentionally would be grossly unethical. But it can, and does, happen by accident. The players may want to check up – and there is nothing more disconcerting than looking for a revoke in a haystack.

**Dummy's Rights.** Incidentally, this is one of the few occasions for dummy to shine. When declarer shows out, dummy can ask: 'Having none?' And dummy can warn declarer if he is about to play from the wrong hand. There is not much else that dummy can do, except order drinks for the other players.

**Fumbling.** Not revoking does not call for great skill, and the subject has not, so far, inspired even one erudite treatise. But this is as good a pretext as any for a piece of wordly-wise advice: sort your cards into suits, and arrange them in sequence. Avoid the hideous habit of fingering every card, in turn, before deciding upon the one you want to play. In short, don't fumble. Get used to thinking first and playing afterwards. Caressing the cardboard and fondling the pips does not help to select the right card.

**Preview.** You now know the movements, the routine and the jargon. So this is a good spot for a preview of the two principal arts that make up the game of bridge: bidding the hand and playing the cards.

**The Purpose of Bidding.** Bidding is the language of partnership – the medium for transmitting and interpreting information. Within the limits of the bidding mechanism, every player at the table endeavours to tell partner about his high cards and distribution – the pattern made by the four suits – and to read partner's message on the same theme.

The game of bridge is played with twenty-six cards against twenty-six cards. Good bidding by the side enables each player to visualize the *combined* values of the partnership; to assess the number of tricks which these values should yield; and to choose the best denomination in which to make them, usually the longest suit.

Like TV, bidding consists in receiving and sending out a picture.

**The Purpose of Play.** No skill is needed to cash ready-made winners – aces and kings that take tricks in their own right. Declarer's object is to develop to the utmost the *potential* value of his twenty-six cards; to synchronize and to exploit the hitting power of his own hand and dummy's. Defenders try to check him, and at the same time to develop their own potential. And it is only a slight exaggeration to say that a player's skill can be measured by the value he extracts from the *small cards*.

For every gambit open to declarer, there is a counter available to the defence. It is a game of thrust and parry in which judgement and technique are the decisive factors. The lessons on play explain the recognized moves, and with each move, the appropriate countermove.

**Diagrams.** At first, you may find it easier to follow these lessons with a pack of cards by your side and to deal every hand as it comes along. It is good practice, too – particularly in not fumbling, and in playing from the right hand. But it takes time. By and by, you will learn to take in the cards at a glance by looking at a diagram on paper. Soon – sooner than you expect – you will familiarize yourself with the symbols. It is a useful habit, and it will come naturally, without any effort on your part. What is more, it will save a lot of time.

The signs never vary. The honour cards are known by their capital initials: A for Ace; K for king; Q for queen; J for jack (Kn, for knave is also popular). The ten alone appears in full – '10'. All the other cards are shown as x's, and it is not uncommon to refer to them by that name.

For the sake of convenience, South – at the bottom of the figure – is always declarer. North is, therefore, dummy, and it invariably falls to West to make the opening lead.

Here is the typical diagram, which you have doubtless seen already in the newspapers:

And now we can get down to real business. Ready? Go!

## Exercises

1. The bidding has followed this course:

| South (dealer) | West | North | East |
|---|---|---|---|
| One club | One heart | No bid | No bid |

If South now says no bid, will West have another bid or will the auction be at an end?

2. South opens the bidding with four spades. West wants to overcall. What is the lowest bid he can make?

3. The bidding has been:

| South (dealer) | West | North | East |
|---|---|---|---|
| One no-trump | No bid | No bid | Double |
| No bid | No bid | | |

Can North redouble or is the bidding over?

4. Declarer, South, leads a trump from dummy.

   (a) In which hand did he win the previous trick?
   (b) Whose turn is it to play?

5. The contract is one club by East. Can you tell what South bid?

6. West has doubled three no-trumps. Can East redouble? Can South?

7. East is the dealer.

   (a) Who shuffles the other pack?
   (b) Who will deal next time?

8. After several rounds of bidding, South calls seven no-trumps, West doubles and North redoubles. What bid, if any, can East make?

9. At which stage does declarer's partner put his hand on the table?

10. The contract is four spades, but declarer's play shows clearly that he imagines the contract to be no-trumps. Can dummy draw attention to his mistake?

# *Part Two*

## LESSON III

# BIDDING

**The Opening Bid.** Bridge players fall into two categories: those who hold average cards; and those who won't admit it.

**The Point Count.** Strength – the capacity to take tricks – has two pillars: The first is high cards. The second is distribution.

Distribution means the shape of the hand and comprises the latent strength of the small cards, which can be developed into winners – especially in the case of a long suit.

To measure both high cards and distribution, use the point count. It is by far the best method of hand valuation for the beginner. And it is often the yardstick of leading players throughout the world.

Count: 4 points for an Ace.  3 points for a King.
2 points for a Queen.  1 point for a Knave.

That means that there are forty points altogether in the pack, – ten in each suit – as far as high cards are concerned. If the strength is divided evenly between the four players at the table, each one will hold ten points. That is the average.

**A Minimum.** To start the auction requires more than that. A bid of one lays claim to seven tricks out of thirteen and demands, therefore, some preponderance of strength.

A minimum opening bid should add up to thirteen points. When you gain experience, you will, occasionally, make do

with less. Meanwhile, stick to thirteen. Anything less may turn
out to be unlucky.

At first sight, the 4–3–2–1 scale seems unsatisfactory, for it
appears to leave distribution out of account. Take an extreme
case and imagine that you are dealt all thirteen cards of a suit.
With that suit as trumps, you cannot fail to win every trick. Yet
in high cards, you hold no more than the average – ten points.

**Points for Length.** Clearly, distributional values call for a
radical adjustment in the count. Just as you open on a preponderance of high cards, so you can also open on preponderance
in distribution. The two sets of values are co-related. And this
is how it works:

To make up the thirteen cards, every hand must contain at
least one four-card suit. Anything over that is an asset – distributionally. A five-card suit is worth *1 point extra*. A six-card
suit, *2 points*. For every *long* card – every card in excess of four
in the same suit – add a point. A second four-card suit is also
worth a point.

And if you have *two* suits with long cards, you write up both.

As you will see from the lessons on play, which follow, the
small cards can be established. Eventually, when the high cards
have fallen, the x's (the cards below the ten) can take tricks.

**Combined Count.** To assess the value of your hand, count the
high cards first, then the distribution.

Try it out:

(a)  ♠ A Q x        (b)  ♠ A Q x x x x
     ♡ Q x x             ♡ A J x
     ♢ K x x             ♢ x x x
     ♣ Q x x             ♣ x

Both (a) and (b) come to thirteen. In (a) the count is made up
of high cards alone. In (b) the two long spades swell by two the
high card strength of eleven.

**Bid on Length, not Strength.** The next question is: *what* suit should you bid? A beginner, tends, normally, to pick the suit with the highest cards. That is wrong. Pick the *longest* suit.

Look at these examples.

♠ A K Q ♠ A K J x
♡ Q 10 x x x ♡ J 10 x x x
◇ K x x ◇ K x
♣ x x ♣ J x

Each time, the best suit is hearts, not spades. In selecting your trump suit be guided by length, and remember that the high cards in the short side-suits will probably take tricks anyway. But those little trumps enable you to *control* the play. That is what trumps are for and that is why you want to have as many of them as you can get – and to leave as few as possible for opponents.

So let it be established as the first principle of bidding that you open on *length*. And since every hand must have a four-card suit, no three-card combination – even A K Q – is considered a normal opening.

**Biddable Suits.** If your hand, as a whole, is good enough to open, you can bid *any* five-card suit, even if it consists of five desultory x's.

And what about the four-card suits? As you gain experience, you will incline increasingly to open on 'bad' four-card suits. It is not really dangerous, but the technique calls for a certain skill. Until you acquire it, take your minimum standard: K 10xx or Q J xx – something headed by the ace or king or *two* of the lesser honours. Later on, you will shade it. But not yet.

Of course, you will often hold hands with thirteen points or more, but no worthwhile suit. Ready to start the auction, you will be pressed for something to say. The best solution, while you are learning, is to bid one no-trump.

**One No-trump.** This has its snags, but time and again, it will solve the problem of the balanced hand. The term 'balanced' describes broadly all those hands which have no singleton (one card only in a suit) and no long suit. On *un*balanced hands – with length and shortages – it is natural to think of a suit contract. But with the even 4–3–3–3 pattern – one four-card suit and three cards in each of the others – and with the 4–4–3–2 shape, think of one no-trump. The 5–3–3–2 type, when the five-card suit is a minor (diamonds or clubs), is also admissible.

In the actual play of the hand, all suits in a no-trump contract are equal. The highest card of the suit led – by either side – wins the trick. Declarer can, therefore, find himself in trouble if the defence hits a weak spot and reels off a five- or six-card suit. Sometimes, it cannot be helped. But it is distinctly unpleasant, and to guard against it the no-trump bidder should try to hold something useful in every suit – some honour card that can stop the run of the enemy's suit. In short, a guard or stopper.

That is one of the snags. Even on balanced hands, every suit is not always guarded. For all that, despite the flaws, the opening bid of one no-trump has many attractions. To grasp them more fully calls for a short digression on bidding in general.

**Opening Promises Rebid.** An opening bid is a means to an end – not an end in itself. The idea is to *get together* with partner – to exchange pictures of the two hands. More often than not the pictures are built up gradually. You bid a suit, revealing one corner of your hand. Partner responds, giving a view of his. On the *second round* you begin to fill in the canvas. And it is taken for granted that there *will be* a second round – that if you open, and your partner responds, you will bid again.

That last statement calls for a few words of explanation. It does not mean that, having opened, you must call again, *come what may*.

In the first place, partner may have *already* passed in the course of the auction. If so, you, too, can pass with an easy conscience. Partner's pass limits his hand. He cannot have a 'whale' – or a 'rock-crusher'. Otherwise he would have opened the bidding. But if partner, having had no chance to speak before, calls *another* suit in response to yours, you are expected to bid again. That is the principle at work. A response in a *different* suit calls for another bid – a rebid – from the opener.

Partner may support your suit. Or his response may take the form of one or more no-trumps. Should either prove to be the case, you can pass.

But the concept of bidding is to explore and to approach. If the opener calls a suit – as distinct from no-trumps – he must be prepared to hear partner call *another* suit. And that will mean that he must bid again.

Knowing that – unless partner passes – he will have another chance to speak, the opening bidder does not rush his fences. He enters the auction with thirteen points. But he may have a good deal more – anything up to twenty or so. And within these limits, the responder is kept in the dark until the *second* round.

**No-trump: a Limited Bid.** This does not apply in the same measure to an opening of one no-trump. The margin between the minimum and the maximum is not so wide. In short, one no-trump is limited. Unlike a suit-bid, its strength is defined within fairly narrow limits. There is no law as to what these limits should be and on this more than one school of thought exists. While you are finding your feet at bridge, keep to the 13–15 standard. On balanced hands – no five-card major and no singleton – open a no-trump with not less than thirteen and not more than fifteen.

It is fashionable these days to play what is known as a 'strong 'no-trump' – 16–18 points. Under the popular Acol system, the strength of the no-trump varies according to vulnerability. It is 12–14 non-vulnerable and 16–18 points vulnerable. There is a lot to be said for it and some of your partners may prefer it. In due course, you may grow to like it yourself. For the present do not let such things worry you. Stick to 13–15. You will hold that sort of hand often enough, and by opening one no-trump you will save yourself the trouble of finding another bid on the second round. This means, in effect, a 'weak' no-trump throughout with a point extra as a safety margin while you gain experience.

It is because a no-trump is relatively fixed in strength, that the opener does *not* guarantee a rebid. If he has a minimum, he passes on the the second round. The reason is that, this time, the first bid gives a *complete picture* and allows partner to size up the situation. He knows your strength within three points and he knows, also, that you must have at least a doubleton (two cards) in any suit he likes to bid.

Partner's detailed reactions will come up for scrutiny in the next lesson, when we come to responses. Meanwhile, note these two salient features of the opening one no-trump:

1. Distribution and strength are conveyed in a single bid.
2. The opener does *not* promise to bid again.

**Opening Bid in a Suit.** Many hands, of course, are not suitable for opening one no-trump. *Shape* is the first consideration. With distributional values, the opener looks for a fit with his partner – a suit *both* like. The emphasis is on quantity, not quality. A good fit implies a lot of trumps – not less than eight between the two hands and more if possible. That leaves opponents with five at most and ensures a working majority for declarer.

With

♠ A J x x x  ♡ K x x  ◇ x  ♣ K Q x x

the opening bid is one spade. And the rebid – over two diamonds, perhaps – will be two spades.

Any suit of five cards or more can be bid *twice* and provides, therefore, a natural rebid.

But keep this point well before you. It is the key to good bidding: before you open, *think of your second round bid*.

**Balanced Hands.** Though no difficulty arises on hands with a five-card suit, the squat, balanced pattern sometimes presents a problem, and one no-trump is not always the way out.

First, the hand may be too strong. If you promise partner 13–15, you will fool him if you make the same bid on 18 or 19. And the whole purpose of the bidding mechanism is to give partner a *true* picture, so that he should know what to do.

Secondly, a no-trump is necessarily vague. To that extent it hinders the search for a good trump suit. You may have been dealt:

♠ A 10 x x   ♡ A K J x   ◇ x x   ♣ Q x x

Partner may have support for one of the majors, but it may well be that his hand, like yours, has no guard in diamonds. Should that be the case, you will make quite a few tricks in spades or hearts – but not in no-trumps.

**Touching Suits.** What, then, is the best bid?

The first impulse is to call one heart, because it is the strongest suit. But to that there is one big objection: it may make life difficult next time – on the rebid.

Unlike five-card suits, a four-card suit is *not* rebiddable. Partner may have a singleton or none, and there is no joy in playing the hand when the other side has most of the trumps.

Over two diamonds, or even two clubs from the responder, you would find yourself in a fix.

What can you do on the second round? Two spades? That

seems all right, but the sequence hearts-first-spades-next has one serious drawback.

Hearing that you have both majors, partner will try to choose the one he likes better – or hates less. If it is spades, all may be well, for he can just pass. But if it is hearts, he will be in a quandary. If he passes, you will not be in your best contract. And if he puts you back to hearts, he will have to call *three*. The rank of the suits gets in the way. To go back from a higher to a lower-ranking suit always means raising the level – contracting for extra tricks.

**Keeping Down the Level.** That is why with two touching suits (spades and hearts; hearts and diamonds; diamonds and clubs) of equal length, the opener calls the higher-ranking suit *first*. On the second round he calls the other, lower-ranking suit. With two 4-card majors this can be awkward, so give preference, whenever possible, to one no-trump. That is the opening bid most experienced players would choose with the hand on the previous page.

A point to bear in mind is that the sequence – one spade, then two hearts – suggests *five* spades.

All in all, with two 4-card majors, don't set out to show both. If partner has already passed, open one heart. He may bid one spade; if not, you needn't bid again.

The same principle applies to two touching five-card suits.

♠ x   ♡ K x x x x   ◇ A K Q x x   ♣ x x

The correct opening is one heart, and the rebid – over either black suit or one no-trump – is two diamonds.

The fact that diamonds are the stronger suit matters little. Preparation for the next round is all-important.

**Opening One Club.** When one of his four-card suits is clubs, the opener is in no difficulty. Being the lowest ranking suit, one club provides a rebid automatically. Over any response at the one level, the second round bid can be one no-trump.

This is the sort of hand you will hold thousands of times:

♠ x x   ♡ K Q x x   ◇ A K x   ♣ Q 10 x x

Without anything in spades, one no-trump is not really advisable. A club is much better. If partner calls a heart, you raise him to two hearts. If he bids a spade, your rebid is one no-trump. Information has been exchanged and you are still not committed to more than seven tricks.

**Thinking Ahead.** Again clubs is not your best suit, and again it does not matter in the least. In fact, clubs are so flexible, so economical in developing the auction, that you can shade your high-card requirements to open one club. Even J x x x will do in your hour of need if it helps to solve the problem of the rebid.

Just how important it is to think one move ahead and to keep down the level, will emerge fully in the next lesson, when we move round the table to look at responder's problems.

## CHART I

### COMBINED COUNT

| HIGH CARDS | DISTRIBUTION |
|---|---|
| Count | Count |
| 4 points for an ace | 1 point for every card in |
| 3 points for a king | excess of four in *each* |
| 2 points for a queen | suit and 1 point for a second |
| 1 point for a knave | four-card suit. |

Add points for distribution to the high card points. The total will show you the strength of your hand.

## CHART II – OPENING BIDS ON WEAK AND INTERMEDIATE HANDS

| High card points | Distribution | What to Open | Prospective Rebid |
|---|---|---|---|
| 11 | One six-card suit or Two five-card suits | One of the six-card suit or If the two suits are touching, one of the *higher-ranking five-card suit* | The same suit again at the two level. The second five-card suit if you can show it at the *two level*. If not, you intend to call the first suit again. |
| 12 | One five-card suit | One of the five-card suit | The same suit again at the two level. If you have a four-card suit, as well, you intend to show it, as long as you can do it at the two level – not otherwise. Or one no-trump (no singleton). |
| 13–15 | Open the bidding regardless of distribution. | One no-trump or One club or One of the *higher ranking* of two touching four-card suits (but see page 36). | This does not guarantee a rebid. You intend to rebid one no-trump or to show another four-card suit, if you can do it at the *one level*. |

When in doubt, shade your requirements for an opening bid with good distribution, but be conservative on balanced hands.

## Exercises

How many points, allowing for high cards and distribution, are the following hands worth?

```
1. ♠ A K Q x x x   2. ♠ A K x      3. ♠ J x x x x x x
   ♡ x                ♡ A K J         ♡ A K x
   ◇ Q x x            ◇ Q x x         ◇ Q x
   ♣ x x x            ♣ J x x x       ♣ x
```

What do you bid, as dealer, on:

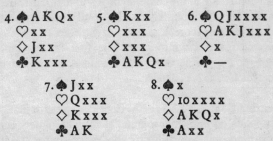

```
4. ♠ A K Q x     5. ♠ K x x       6. ♠ Q J x x x x
   ♡ x x            ♡ x x x           ♡ A K J x x x
   ◇ J x x          ◇ x x x           ◇ x
   ♣ K x x x        ♣ A K Q x         ♣ —
```

```
7. ♠ J x x       8. ♠ x
   ♡ Q x x x        ♡ 10 x x x x
   ◇ K x x x        ◇ A K Q x
   ♣ A K            ♣ A x x
```

9. After two passes, what do you bid on:

```
(a) ♠ A J 10 x   (b) ♠ A K x     (c) ♠ A Q 10 x x
    ♡ x x x          ♡ Q x x          ♡ —
    ◇ K Q J          ◇ A Q J          ◇ K J x x x
    ♣ Q 10 x         ♣ J x x x        ♣ K x x
```

10. What do you bid, in any position, on:

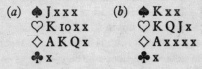

```
(a) ♠ J x x x     (b) ♠ K x x
    ♡ K 10 x x        ♡ K Q J x
    ◇ A K Q x         ◇ A x x x x
    ♣ x               ♣ x
```

# LESSON IV
# BIDDING

**Responses.** Responder starts with an advantage. Since partner opened the bidding, he can already locate on his side 13 of the 40 points in the pack. That applies to high cards only, leaving distribution out of account. But it is a good foundation, none the less.

What is the next step? It is to tell partner how much responder can contribute to the common pool – in high card strength, and also in distribution. That will help to identify the target. Should it be a part score, a game or maybe even a slam?

Two factors come into play. The first is the combined strength of the partnership. The second is a fit – a denomination which suits *both* hands.

**Measuring Combined Strength.** Consider strength first. With all 40 points on one side, a grand slam is absolutely certain. And with 20, one side will probably make six tricks and the other seven. That is a generalization, but it points the way.

**26 and 34.** As a rough and ready measure, it takes a fraction under three points to win a trick. To size up your expectations keep two figures in mind: 26 and 34.

On evenly balanced hands, it takes just about 26 points to make a game. And it needs 34 for a small slam. As you progress, so you will tend to scale down these requirements by about 1 point in each case. But for the present, assess your expectations on the basis of 26 and 34.

Responder's technique lies in adding his values to partner's. Sometimes it takes several rounds of bidding to reach the total. Sometimes the goal – the final contract – comes into view at once. The quickest result is obtained when partner opens one no-trump.

**Responding to a No-trump.** As we learned in the last lesson, a no-trump promises a balanced hand with 13–15 points. As responder you hold:

| | | |
|---|---|---|
| ♠ A x x | | ♠ Q x x |
| ♡ K J x | or | ♡ K x x |
| ♢ Q x x x | | ♢ K Q x x x |
| ♣ K x x | | ♣ Q x |

What is your first reaction? Satisfaction, surely, for before the cards are dealt again your side should be a game up. Even if partner started with a minimum, the combined values add up to 26.

**A Game Signal.** There is another way of looking at it without bringing in arithmetic. If partner opens, and you have the values to open yourself, that shows that you have enough for game between you. And there is no need to beat about the bush.

The bidding goes:

| *Opener* | *Responder* |
|---|---|
| One no-trump | Three no-trumps |

It is so much easier to make nine tricks in no-trumps than eleven in diamonds or clubs, that responder does not, normally, mention a long minor. He just raises partner for all he is worth in *no-trumps*. If, assuming a minimum (13 points) opposite, the total comes to 26 or more, he calls three.

With 11 or 12, he bids two no-trumps. That tells the opener to go game, if he started with *more* than the minimum. Not otherwise.

And with less than 11, the response to partner's no-trump is – pass. For even opposite a maximum 15 the *combined* total must fall short of the required 26.

That is what a limited bid looks like from the receiving end. It tells so much of the story that responder can generally write the final chapter on his own.

**Suit Responses Over No-trumps.** Of course, the contract does not have to be no-trumps just because partner opens a no-trump. It all depends on responder's *shape*. If he has a long major and a singleton or a void (total absence of a suit), a suit contract may be preferable.

                1. ♠ K J x x x x      2. ♠ —
                   ♡ x          or        ♡ A x x x x x
                   ◇ A J x x               ◇ Q J 10 x x
                   ♣ K x                   ♣ A x

Four spades is the response on 1 and four hearts on 2.

Observe that, once more, there is no beating about the bush. Responder knows that his side has enough strength for Game. And he knows that he will find opposite at least a doubleton in his suit. With a six-card major he can reckon on eight trumps or more between the two hands, and that is good enough.

**Consulting the Opener.** With a *five*-card major it is best to refer the question to the opener. The bid is *three* spades (or *three* hearts). The no-trump bidder calls four if he has three cards in that suit, and rebids three no-trumps if his holding in partner's major is a doubleton.

            Opener              Responder
            ♠ J x x             ♠ K 10 x x x
            ♡ K J x             ♡ x
            ◇ A Q x x           ◇ K J x
            ♣ K x x             ♣ A Q x x

and the bidding sequence is:

            Opener              Responder
            One no-trump        Three spades
            Four spades

But change one of the opener's small spades into a club and

he would rebid three no-trumps. Any rebid by opener other than four spades or three no-trumps – e.g. four diamonds – is known as a *cue bid*, shows an ace – *not* a suit – and hints at a slam, agreeing responder's suit, if he is interested. That, however, is for next year – or the year after.

**A Forcing Bid.** Can the opener pass? Emphatically no. A single jump – from one no-trump to three in a suit – is *forcing*. It is *unlimited*. That is to say that it shows a strong hand, but does not disclose *how* strong.

A forcing bid can *never* be passed. Hence the expression. We shall have more to say about forcing bids in the next lesson but it may be stated now, for all time, that partner is obliged to find another call. The player who forces, takes all responsibility, and it follows that to do so he must have a very strong hand.

**Weakness Take Out.** Sometimes responder is weak, but prefers a suit contract to no-trumps. His hand may be:

$$(a) \quad \spadesuit Q J x x x x \quad (b) \quad \spadesuit x$$
$$\heartsuit x \qquad \text{or} \qquad \heartsuit Q x x$$
$$\diamondsuit J x x \qquad \qquad \diamondsuit A Q x x x$$
$$\clubsuit x x x \qquad \qquad \clubsuit x x x x$$

So he calls two spades on (*a*) and two diamonds on (*b*). He does not expect to make his contract on (*a*). But he promises length – at least a five-card suit. And he tells the opener that more tricks can probably be made in his suit than in no-trumps.

To respond two in a suit – a minor or a major – over partner's no-trump is known as a weakness take out. The bid can be *weaker* than a pass and the opener must not rebid, even if his no-trump is a maximum.

**No-trump Responses: a Summary.** This, then, is responder's technique when partner opens a no-trump:

He adds the *combined* strength of the two hands, and more often than not, announces the result straight away – 'Four hearts', 'No bid', 'Three no-trumps', or whatever it may be.

If the decision is likely to be close, depending on whether the opener has a minimum or a maximum, responder calls two no-trumps.

With a weak distributional hand, responder calls two of his longest suit.

And with a strong hand, but only a five-card major, the best response is a jump to three, announcing game values, but leaving partner to decide whether the hand is to be played in the major or in no-trumps.

**Stayman.** Before leaving the no-trump theme mention should be made of a convention in universal use named after the American master Sam Stayman. This is an artificial bid of two clubs over one no-trump, the purpose being to bring to light a 4–4 major suit fit, which might otherwise be lost. Opener bids his 4-card major, if he has one, and two diamonds if he hasn't. That, again, is artificial, having no bearing on diamonds as a suit.

This is how the convention works. Partner opens one no-trump and you hold:

| (a) ♠ J x x x | (b) ♠ Q x x x | (c) ♠ K 10 |
|---|---|---|
| ♡ Q x x x | ♡ J 10 x x x | ♡ A x x x |
| ◇ J x x x | ◇ x | ◇ A x |
| ♣ x | ♣ K x x | ♣ 10 x x x x |

Each time, you call two clubs hoping to hear a major from your partner. If he has none and calls two diamonds, it should still prove a better spot than one no-trump on (a). Whatever he says you pass.

On (b) you will pass two spades and call two hearts over two diamonds, the bid you would have made directly without Stayman. Now opener passes, for you have promised no strength at all, only five hearts and four (or five) spades.

On (c) the bid over two diamonds is two no-trumps. You make the same bid over two spades; but should you hear two hearts you are worth a raise to four hearts, your two doubletons making up the required strength. Three hearts would be invitational, but not forcing.

Now for stronger holdings:

(d) ♠ K J 10 x      (e) ♠ K x x
    ♡ A x x          ♡ A J x x x
    ◇ K Q          ◇ A J
    ♣ 10 x x x          ♣ A Q

On (d) your bid is four spades over two spades and three no-trumps over two diamonds or two hearts.

On (e) you are worth six over a response in either major. Over two diamonds jump to three hearts, which is forcing, but if opener bids three no-trumps, denying 3-card heart support, pass. He could have:

(i) ♠ A x x x      (ii) ♠ A x x
    ♡ K Q x x          ♡ K x
    ◇ x x          ◇ K x x x
    ♣ K x x          ♣ K x x x

Opposite (i) you would be unlucky not to make a slam in spades or hearts, but on a diamond lead you wouldn't make six no-trumps.

With (ii) opposite there's no reasonable prospect of a slam anywhere.

There are many variations and adornments, but that is the essence of Stayman. You needn't bother with the convention for a while yet, but when you gain experience and come to use it, always remember to think a move ahead. Don't bid two clubs until you know what you intend to do next, whether opener has a 4-card major or not.

**Responding to a Suit Bid.** A suit opening is not limited, like a no-trump, and calls for different treatment by responder. Since the margin of strength can be as much as 7 points – from 13 to 20 – responder tries to keep the bidding open on as little as 6. Experienced players may do it on less. The opener *may* have 20, and then the side should be in game.

**The Cheapest Bid.** The next question is *what* responder should say. A long suit speaks for itself. But all too often he will hold a balanced hand with 6–8 points. That is the time to make the *cheapest* bid – to keep down the level.

The cheapest bid is the one which takes up least bidding space. Over a club it is a diamond. Over a heart, a spade. And over a spade, one no-trump.

Again, you don't call your best suit as a matter of course.

The opening is a heart and you hold:

<table>
<tr><td>1.</td><td>♠ Q 10 x x<br>♡ x x<br>◇ A Q x x<br>♣ x x x</td><td>or</td><td>2.</td><td>♠ K 10 x x<br>♡ x x<br>◇ K J x x x<br>♣ x x</td></tr>
</table>

The correct response is one spade on both hands. Why? Because two diamonds would raise the level, and with a weak hand it is best to be modest.

**Constructive Bids.** There is another reason. To show a major is always more *constructive*. If opponents enter the auction, your side can outbid anything they call with spades *at the same level*. And if partner is very good and it is a question of game, ten tricks in a major is an easier proposition than eleven in a minor.

The opener always calls his *longest* suit first. Responder does not. In bridge the goose and the gander demand different sauces.

The opener has time to show two suits. Responder may not want to speak more than once. On a weak hand, he strives to convey the most important information and expects to keep silent thereafter.

With less than 10–11 points responder should call a four-card major rather than a five-card minor. With more, he can call the minor first, and the shorter major on the next round.

Note the emphasis on the level. Making eight tricks is more difficult than making seven. On a minimum, 6–8 points, responder tries to keep the bidding down to one of something. If he calls two, he must have a little over a minimum, say, 9 points.

Responder holds:

♠ K 10 x x ♡ x x ◇ A x x x x ♣ x x

If partner opens one club, the response is one diamond. That is the natural bid, for diamonds is the longest suit.

But over one heart, the response is one spade. The hand is too weak to raise the auction to the level of two.

There is nothing artificial about it. The idea is to be cautious with poor cards – and to make the cheapest bid. The corollary is that when a player does *not* make a cheap bid – when he raises the level – he must have some extra values.

**Responding One No-trump.** Sometimes responder can show no suit at all. He is just good enough to keep the auction going, but he has no four-card suit that can be shown at the one level. His partner opens one spade and he holds

    (a) ♠ 10 x x      (b) ♠ x x
        ♡ x x x   or   ♡ J x x
        ◇ Q 10 x       ◇ K x x
        ♣ A J x x     ♣ Q x x x x

The bid is one no-trump. This shows a balanced hand – though it does not exclude a five-card minor – and a strength of not more than 8–10 points, but probably less. Remember that. If you respond one no-trump with more than 10 points, you may easily miss game, for the opener will pass on as much as 16. A response of one no-trump always proclaims *weakness*.

In response, as in opening, all no-trump bids are limited – with a narrow margin between the minimum and the maximum. Therefore, partner does *not* have to bid again.

**Jump Responses in No-trumps.** On a balanced hand of 11–12 points, the response is *two* no-trumps. And with 13–15 the bid is *three* no-trumps.

The opener calls one heart and you hold:

|   | 1. | | 2. | |
|---|---|---|---|---|
|   | ♠ K J x | | ♠ A x x | |
|   | ♡ J x x | | ♡ Q x | |
|   | ◇ K 10 x | | ◇ K x x x | |
|   | ♣ Q J x x | | ♣ K x x x | |

You call two no-trumps. If partner has a minimum he passes. With more he bids game.

|   | 3. | | 4. | |
|---|---|---|---|---|
|   | ♠ A J x | | ♠ A Q x | |
|   | ♡ J x x | | ♡ Q x | |
|   | ◇ K 10 x | | ◇ K x x x | |
|   | ♣ A x x x | | ♣ K J x x | |

This time the response is three no-trumps. Even opposite a minimum the two hands add up to 26 or more. Don't call two when you are good enough for three. Partner may pass and you will miss a game.

**Finding a Fit.** We now come to the problem of finding a fit – a contract which suits both hands *distributionally*.

If a player has long hearts and no spades, while his partner has long spades and no hearts, much of the side's strength is wasted. The aces and kings will take tricks, but it will be difficult to develop the small cards.

Conversely, when both partners like the same suit, the strength of the two hands expands.

**Raising Partner's Major.** Often the fit is apparent at once. When responder has four cards in the opener's major, the search for the right denomination is over. It becomes only a question of how many tricks the side can make. That turns on strength and the 26 formula applies as usual. You can reckon up the values as before and you will not go far wrong. But there is a more precise measure for assessing responder's strength once a *fit has been established*. Like everything else in bridge, it is founded on logic, and with a little experience, you will be able to work it out on your own.

Having decided that, with four or more cards in support, you like partner's suit, pass to the question: What else, besides the trumps, does partner hope to find in your hand? The answer is: shortages. He will be mighty pleased to see a void, and next to that, a singleton.

If declarer has, say, two small clubs and you have none at all, he will be able to ruff both his losing clubs in dummy. And should you have a singleton, it will still be worth a trick to him, for he will lose one club and trump the other.

Even a doubleton is not without value. Partner may have three small cards in the same suit or A x x, maybe, and if so, he will make a trick out of your hand by ruffing.

Try it the other way. The worst hand in support of partner's suit, distributionally, is a 4–3–3–3 pattern. You have four trumps, but nothing for them to ruff.

Having found a fit in a major, take points for shortages, adding:

> 3 for a Void.
> 2 for a Singleton.
> 1 for a Doubleton.

As you gain confidence, so you will be inclined, at times, to write up these figures. And you will be quite right. But the hour has not struck, and meanwhile, the 1–2–3 scale will prove a faithful guide.

To assess the worth of your hand in support of partner's major, add the points – for high cards and for shortages. It is not very different from adding points for length, but a little more accurate in practice.

Having reached your total, raise partner's major to the limit. The better you are, the more you bid – up to game level.

Some holdings are so powerful, that they call for more forceful measures. We will come to them later. For the present we are concerned with hands which justify raising the level by one, two or three. Let us try out a few.

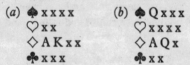

*Opener*     *Responder*
One spade    Two spades

That is a minimum raise, showing 6–9 points and as a rule four spades, but perhaps three to an honour. It could be:

   (a) ♠ x x x x     (b) ♠ Q x x x
       ♡ x x             ♡ x x x x
       ♢ A K x x       ♢ A Q x
       ♣ x x x         ♣ x x

A single raise – from one to two – is also in order on:

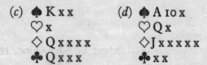

   (c) ♠ K x x       (d) ♠ A 10 x
       ♡ x                ♡ Q x
       ♢ Q x x x x      ♢ J x x x x x
       ♣ Q x x x       ♣ x x

The absence of a fourth spade is truly regrettable, but the singleton in (c) and the two doubletons in (d) make up for it. Partner should be able to make a trick or two by ruffing.

Besides, showing the diamonds is not constructive.

In no circumstances should partner's suit be raised on a doubleton, whether it is x x or A K. A suit bid promises nothing longer than four cards. If responder has a doubleton, that may leave defenders with a preponderance of trumps. And why select as trumps a suit in which the enemy enjoys numerical superiority?

The picture changes if partner *rebids* his suit. That shows five at least, and though a doubleton still provides poor trump support, it will do at a pinch.

In short, raise partner's major always on four, sometimes on three, but never on less – until he rebids it.

**Jump Raises.** With four of partner's major and 11–12 points, respond three. And with 13–15 points, the bid is four. Count the points for high cards – and for shortages.

|   | 1. | | 2. | |
|---|---|---|---|---|
| | ♠ J x x | | ♠ A x x | |
| | ♡ Q x x x | | ♡ x x x x | |
| | ♢ x | | ♢ A x | |
| | ♣ A K x x x | | ♣ K x x | |

Over a heart from partner call three hearts.
And with

|   | 3. | | 4. | |
|---|---|---|---|---|
| | ♠ A K x x x x | | ♠ A K Q J | |
| | ♡ K J x x | | ♡ 10 x x x | |
| | ♢ x | | ♢ A x x | |
| | ♣ x x | | ♣ x x | |

respond four hearts.

Once a fit has been established in one major, there is no purpose in showing the other.

**Responding to a Minor.** This does not apply to the minors. Partner calls one club and you hold:

(a) ♠ Q x x          (b) ♠ A J x x
    ♡ K J x x            ♡ x x
    ◇ x x               ◇ K x
    ♣ Q x x x           ♣ J x x x x

Call a heart on (a) and a spade on (b). The opener may have a fit for your major, and if he is strong, you may even make game.

Should he rebid one no-trump, you can bid two clubs – especially on (b).

Comparatively few game contracts are played in the minors. That is why, knowing that over a response in a new suit the opener will speak again, it is worth using up a round of bidding to explore the position in the majors. It is so much easier to make ten tricks than eleven.

But you see now how useful is the opener's promise of a rebid. It gives the partnership time and space to look for the best contract.

And now we return to the opener. Let us watch him, in the next lesson, rebid over the responses we have been making in this one.

## CHART III

### TARGETS IN BIDDING

If your side has a combined strength of:

| | | |
|---|---|---|
| 22–25 points | your holding warrants a | Part Score Contract |
| 26 points | your holding warrants a | Game Contract |
| 34 points | you are in the | Slam Zone |

## CHART IV – RESPONSES

| Distributional and high card strength | Responder's alternatives | Determining factors |
|---|---|---|
| 0–5 | No bid | |
| 6–8 | Show a suit<br>or<br>One no-trump<br>or<br>Single raise for partner | Without a fit for partner, you call your suit, if it is biddable, providing that you can do it at the *one level*. Otherwise, call: one no-trump. With four cards in partner's major<br>or<br>three cards in support, and a doubleton or singleton, raise him by one (e.g. 1 heart–2 hearts). |
| 9–10 | Show a suit, if possible | Bid your suit at the two level, if necessary, but you can still respond one no-trump with 10 points. Over one spade, two hearts promises a 5-card suit.<br>With a fit for partner's major, raise him by one on 9 points. Holding 10 points it is touch and go. If you can stretch it, raise his suit to three (e.g. 1 heart–3 hearts). |
| 11–12 | Show your suit<br>or<br>Two no-trumps<br>or<br>Jump raise (to three) in partner's suit | Always show a biddable major over a minor.<br>With a balanced hand and something in every suit, call two no-trumps.<br>Holding four cards (or more) in partner's suit, raise him to three. |
| 13–15 | Show a suit<br>or<br>Three no-trumps<br>or<br>Raise partner's major to game | All the above principles apply, but unless you decide to show a suit of your own, bid *game* – in no-trumps or in partner's suit, according to shape. |

When you have found a fit with partner, assess your distributional strength, not by counting long cards (in excess of four in every suit), but by asking points for shortages. The scale: 3 points for a void – 2 points for a singleton – 1 point for a doubleton.

## Exercises

Your partner opens one no-trump. What do you call on:

| 1. | 2. | 3. | 4. |
|---|---|---|---|
| ♠ x x | ♠ A x x | ♠ x x | ♠ A J 10 x x |
| ♡ x x | ♡ x x x | ♡ J 10 x x x x | ♡ Q x |
| ◇ J x x | ◇ K Q x x | ◇ Q x x x | ◇ J x x |
| ♣ A K Q J x x | ♣ Q 10 x | ♣ x | ♣ A J x |

Your partner opens one club. What do you respond on:

| 5. | 6. | 7. | 8. |
|---|---|---|---|
| ♠ A x x | ♠ K x x | ♠ A x x | ♠ K x x |
| ♡ K x x | ♡ Q J x x | ♡ x x | ♡ K 10 x |
| ◇ J 10 x x | ◇ x x | ◇ K x x | ◇ Q J x |
| ♣ K x x | ♣ A J x x | ♣ K J x x x | ♣ K x x x |

Your partner opens one heart. What do you call on:

| 9. | | 10. | |
|---|---|---|---|
| ♠ A Q x x x | | ♠ Q x | |
| ♡ J x x x | | ♡ 10 x x x | |
| ◇ x | | ◇ x | |
| ♣ A J x | | ♣ K J x x x x | |

Partner opens one diamond. What do you respond on:

| 11. | 12. | 13. |
|---|---|---|
| ♠ x x x | ♠ x x x | ♠ x x |
| ♡ K 10 x x | ♡ K 10 x x | ♡ x x x |
| ◇ x | ◇ A J x x | ◇ K x x x x |
| ♣ K 10 x x x | ♣ x x | ♣ A K x |

Partner opens one spade. What do you respond on:

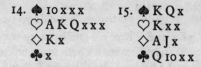

14. ♠ 10 x x x     15. ♠ K Q x
    ♡ A K Q x x x      ♡ K x x
    ◇ K x             ◇ A J x
    ♣ x              ♣ Q 10 x x

# LESSON V

# BIDDING

**Rebids.** The first flirtatious round is at an end. The tentative approaches are over. Now, on the second round of bidding, the players come into the open and announce their real intentions. Whither are they bound? Part score, game or slam?

I opened one club. You, my partner, responded one diamond. How good are we? No one can tell. I might have 13 to your 6. That would give us 19 points out of the 40 and leave opponents with the preponderance of strength.

But, to take an extreme case, I may have 20 to your 15, which would put us well in the slam zone.

**Limiting the Unlimited.** There is a gulf between our minimum and maximum holdings, because we both made unlimited bids. This gulf will now be bridged, for the second round limits the unlimited.

It is my turn first. What should I do over your response of one diamond?

**Showing a Minimum.** With a minimum, I rebid one no-trump or two clubs. Both bids denote the same strength – or rather, lack of strength. The only difference is that a no-trump rebid shows a balanced hand, whereas a suit rebid promises at least a five-card suit and may suggest an unbalanced hand, unsuitable for no-trumps.

I could have

     1.  ♠ K x x    2.  ♠ Q x x
         ♡ K Q x  or   ♡ K Q x
         ♢ x x x        ♢ x
         ♣ A J x x      ♣ A x x x x x

On 1, my rebid is one no-trump, and on 2, two clubs.

And how about you? You could have responded one diamond on any of the following hands:

    (*a*) ♠ K x x  (*b* ♠ A K x  (*c*) ♠ x x x x
        ♡ 10 x x    ♡ x x       ♡ x
        ♢ Q J x x   ♢ Q J x x  ♢ A Q x x x x
        ♣ x x x     ♣ K Q x x   ♣ x x

On (*a*) you nearly passed. Now, on the second round, you say no bid with an easy conscience.

With (*b*) the fact that my rebid of one no-trump shows a minimum does not perturb you in the least. Adding your 15 to my 13 you can still see enough for game – 2 points more, in fact. Having a balanced hand, no-trumps is the obvious contract. So you bid three no-trumps.

What of (c)? It is not a scintillating collection, but it looks as if it will yield more tricks in diamonds than in anything else – especially if my rebid is one no-trump and not two clubs. Remember, in no-trumps even a rebid promises a balanced hand – no singleton. So you call two diamonds.

There is another way of showing a minimum opening – a single raise in partner's suit. With that we will deal in a page or two.

**Rebid on Good Hands.** Because the rebid by the opener of one no-trump or two of his suit announces a minimum, the same rebid must *not* be made on better hands. The range for a minimum is the same as for an opening no-trump – 13–15. Holding more – jump.

With a balanced pattern and a count of 17–18, the rebid is *two no-trumps*. With 16, look for an alternative, preferably another suit. If you have none, treat 16 as 15 or 17, stretching a point with a 5-card suit and a couple of 10s. With 19–20, the rebid is three no-trumps.

Responder assumes the average and puts up partner's two no-trump rebid to three on 9.

Occasionally, this will mean having to make nine tricks on 25 points only. Even that will come off part of the time, and anyway it is no tragedy to go one down when the alternative is to miss a good chance of game.

**Pass, Sign Off or Game?** On a good distributional hand responder still bids game, of course, though probably not in no-trumps. Take this sequence:

| *Opener* | *Responder* |
|---|---|
| One diamond | One spade |
| Two no-trumps | ? |

Responder holds:

(a) ♠ A J x x   (b) ♠ A J x x x x (c) ♠ A J 10 x x x
    ♡ x x           ♡ x x             ♡ A x
    ◇ J x x         ◇ J x x           ◇ J x x
    ♣ J x x x       ♣ x x             ♣ x x

Knowing that partner has a balanced hand worth 16–18 points, what action should he take?

On (a) he passes. A queen more and the hand would warrant three no-trumps.

On (b) there is still not enough for game. The hand is no better than (a). But spades clearly make for a more attractive contract than no-trumps and the bid is *three spades*.

This is known as a sign off. It is the same idea as a weakness take out over one no-trump and tells partner *to pass*.

Study the logic of the situation. All no-trump rebids are limited. Therefore, after the second round bid of two no-trumps, responder knows how good a hand there is opposite. So it is for him to decide on the final contract.

With a better hand like (c) responder must not call three spades, but *four*. As in the case of an opening no-trump, responder's task is to add the combined values and announce the result.

**A Two-suiter.** Holding a two-suiter he can ask the opener which suit he likes best.

On:

♠ A J x x   ♡ K J x x x   ◇ x x   ♣ x

the sequence would be:

|          | *Opener*        | *Responder*   |
|----------|-----------------|---------------|
|          | One diamond     | One spade     |
|          | Two no-trumps   | Three *hearts* |

Could this be confused with a sign off? No. To call a *new* suit over a two no-trump rebid is encouraging. Only a rebid in the *same* suit at the lowest level (three) shows weakness.

**Action over Three No-trumps Rebid.** The same reasoning inspires responder's actions over the still stronger rebid (19–20) of three no-trumps by the opener. He adds and announces, as before.

|   | *Opener*        | *Responder*   |
|---|-----------------|---------------|
|   | One club        | One spade     |
|   | Three no-trumps | Four spades   |

Responder could have (*a*) or (*b*) below, but *not* (*c*):

| (*a*) ♠ Q 10 x x x x | (*b*) ♠ A Q x x x x | (*c*) ♠ A Q x x x x |
|----------------------|---------------------|---------------------|
| ♡ x                  | ♡ x                 | ♡ x                 |
| ♢ K x x              | ♢ K x x             | ♢ K Q x             |
| ♣ x x x              | ♣ x x x             | ♣ Q x x             |

All three hands should yield more tricks in spades than in no-trumps. But (*c*) is *too good* for four spades. Opposite partner's big hand there should be a slam about, and responder is the one to bid it. The opener has done his bit – his big bit. Responder's hand is still wrapped in mystery. All he has done was to call one spade, an unlimited bid, which could consist of 6 miserable points.

What it amounts to is this: the opener can only see his own hand. His partner can 'see' both. So he must decide.

**Jump Rebids in a Suit.** To show a strong *distributional* hand the opener jumps in his suit on the second round.

He opens one heart on:

♠ A   ♡ K Q J x x x   ◇ A Q x   ♣ x x x

Over a response of one spade the rebid is three hearts – one more than necessary. Add another heart or the knave of diamonds, and the rebid will be four hearts.

Don't jump to three hearts if you are good enough for four. Partner may pass and a game can be easily missed. A jump in the same suit is never forcing. Of course, a jump from one to three is encouraging. But it is no more than that.

Single and double jumps in the same suit follow the principle of no-trump rebids. The better you are, the more you bid. And it is the same scale of values. With 16–18 jump once – one spade, then three spades. With 19–20 the rebid – over, say, two diamonds – is four spades.

This sequence shows, of course, a good, long suit – usually six or seven cards.

**Raising Responder's Suit.** Direct raises in responder's suit follow the same pattern. They are limited; there is a narrow margin between the minimum and maximum. They are quantitative; you raise all you are worth immediately.

To your opening club partner responds one spade. You hold:

| 1. | ♠ K x x x | 2. | ♠ K x x x | 3. | ♠ K x x x |
|---|---|---|---|---|---|
| | ♡ A x | | ♡ A K | | ♡ A Q |
| | ◇ 10 x x | | ◇ x x x | | ◇ A x x |
| | ♣ A Q x x | | ♣ A Q 10 x | | ♣ A Q x x |

Since 1 is a minimum you call two spades, which is no stronger than one no-trump.

On 2 the bid is three spades, and on 3 four spades.

With four of his suit, always raise responder's major *immediately*. The quest for a fit is over. All you have to decide is how many tricks you are likely to make.

As you can see from the examples above, the scale of values is the same as with no-trump rebids and jump rebids in the opener's suit.

A single raise – from one to two – shows a minimum opening, i.e. 13–15 points. The 16–18 hand is worth one jump – from one to three. With more, the opener goes straight to game – four hearts or four spades.

To venture further, over a single raise, responder needs quite a lot – not less than 12 points.

A jump raise is obviously encouraging, but with an absolute minimum responder passes. Anything around 9 points is enough to bid game.

**Opener Changes Suit.** Speaking statistically, most of the situations in bridge fall in one or other of the catergories examined above. On the second round, the opener limits his hand in one of three ways:

He rebids one or more no-trumps.

He rebids his own suit.

He raises responder's suit.

Responder finds it relatively easy to choose the final contract, because he knows within 2 or 3 points the strength of the hand opposite.

At times, the opener cannot supply such accurate information, even on the second round.

Assume that over one heart partner responds two clubs, and the opener has:

|  |  |  |
|---|---|---|
| 1. ♠ Q x x | 2. ♠ Q x | 3. ♠ K x |
| ♡ A Q x x | ♡ A 10 x x x | ♡ A Q x x x |
| ◇ A J x x | ◇ A Q x x | ◇ A K x x x |
| ♣ x x | ♣ J x | ♣ x |

The third hand is much better than the other two, but there is no good alternative to a two diamonds rebid on all three.

**Preference.** How then, should responder react? A change of suit is not limited. But neither is it forcing. With a minimum responder can pass. His primary obligation is to give preference – to tell partner which of his two suits he prefers.

A pass still shows preference – for the last bid suit.

If partner bids hearts, then diamonds, responder passes *only if he has more diamonds* than hearts. With the same length in the red suits he goes back to hearts. The opener may have more hearts than diamonds, but it can hardly be the other way round.

Simple preference *never* shows additional strength.

The sequence is:

| Opener | Responder |
|---|---|
| One heart | Two clubs |
| Two diamonds | ? |

Responder holds:

| (a) ♣ x x x | (b) ♣ x x x | (c) ♠ J x x |
|---|---|---|
| ♡ x x x | ♡ K J | ♡ A x x |
| ◇ K x | ◇ x x x | ◇ x x |
| ♣ A J x x x | ♣ A J x x x | ♣ A Q x x x |

On (a) he calls two hearts; on (b) he passes. But on (c) mere preference is not enough. The bid should be *three* hearts – a jump preference. On both (a) and (b) a one no-trump response might have been preferable.

**Jump Preference.** It is a common fault with beginners to forget that partner will not give them credit for a fair hand if they put him back to his first suit at the *same level*.

With the bidding sequence as above, responder

on (d) ♣ 10 x x x   ♡ x   ◇ x x   ♣ A K J x x x

calls three clubs. Preference does not exclude common sense, and a good six-card suit can rebid at the three level.

**Opener Forces.** The opener's hand may be so strong that, after any response from partner on the first round, he does not want the auction to stop under game. He may have a 19–20 count, but with a distributional hand he may be unable to select immediately the best contract.

To make certain that responder finds another bid, even on the barest minimum, the opener jumps in a new suit. That is *unconditionally forcing to game*, and by ensuring another round of bidding, it gives the opener additional room for manoeuvre.

The opener's hand is:

♠ A K Q x x   ♡ A Q 10 x   ◇ K J x   ♣ x

Partner responds two diamonds to one spade and it is long odds that the side can make game. But what in? Responder would have bid two diamonds on:

| 1. | | 2. | | 3. |
|----|----|----|----|----|
| ♠ J x x | | ♠ x x | | ♠ x x |
| ♡ J x | or | ♡ J x x x | or | ♡ K x |
| ◇ A Q J 10 x | | ◇ A Q 10 x x | | ◇ Q x x x x |
| ♣ x x x | | ♣ K x | | ♣ K Q x x |

To gather more information, and to make sure that responder does not pass on a minimum, the opener forces. Over two clubs he jumps to *three* hearts.

Partner calls three spades on 1; four hearts on 2; and three no-trumps on 3.

With:

♠ x   ♡ x x   ◇ Q 10 x x x x x   ♣ A J x

he will call four diamonds. The opener will bid five – and conceivably six.

**Responder Forces.** Forcing bids are an especially useful weapon in responder's armoury. They enable him to show *values in excess* of the maximum (15) for a direct raise to game – in a suit or in no-trumps.

Essentially unlimited, a forcing bid by responder tells his partner: 'I have a very good hand – enough for game, even if your opening is a minimum. We may easily have a slam, too. Keep the auction *going* and let me know two things: your distribution, and whether you have any extra strength.'

The opening is one heart and responder has

| (a) | ♠ A x | (b) | ♠ A K Q J x x |
| | ♡ K Q x x x | | ♡ K x |
| | ◇ Q 10 x x | | ◇ A x x |
| | ♣ A J | | ♣ K x |

On (a) he calls *three* diamonds and on (b) *two* spades.

Of course (a) will be played in hearts eventually. Even if the opener raises diamonds, responder will go back to hearts. But only by forcing – jumping one round in another suit – can he convey to partner that he is *too good* for an immediate raise to four hearts.

Hand (b) is much better than (a) and will certainly be played in a slam – possibly in a grand slam. But responder would like to hear more about the opener's values. And there is no hurry, for a force – by either opener or responder – ensures that the bidding will not die down till game is reached.

**Rebid Over a Force.** To show that he started with a minimum, the opener rebids his own suit at the lowest level – if his suit is rebiddable – or calls no-trumps. In fact, he uses the same tactics as if the response were at the one level.

But the opener, too, knows that the bidding will be kept going to game. So he can take his time.

|                | *Opener*    | *Responder*   |
|                | One heart   | Three clubs   |
|                | Three hearts| Four hearts   |

The opener can have:

|     |               |     |               |
|-----|---------------|-----|---------------|
| 1.  | ♠ A J x       | 2.  | ♠ A Q x       |
|     | ♡ Q x x x x x or |  | ♡ A K Q x x   |
|     | ◇ K J x       |     | ◇ K J x       |
|     | ♣ x           |     | ♣ x x         |

The three-heart rebid can be good or bad. The difference need not emerge till later, because there is bound to be one more round. Responder must say something.

On 1, the opener has no slam ambitions, and if responder calls four hearts, he will pass happily.

On 2, three hearts is a 'waiting bid'.

Whatever the next bid, the opener will take further action.

**When a Force is not a Force.** All forcing bids are subject to two conditions:

A jump in a new suit by a player who has *already passed*, is *not* forcing. Why? Because the pass limits the hand. It must have *less* strength than an opening. Therefore, partner knows the maximum that he can expect to find opposite and may decide that it is not enough for game.

**Pre-emptive Bids.** Now for the second condition: only a *single* jump (One heart – *two* spades or one diamond – *three* clubs) is a force.

A *double* jump (one heart – *three* spades) is almost the opposite. It shows a long suit, but a weak hand. The idea is to make life harder for opponents.

The same holds true of all pre-emptive bids, as they are known. Opening bids of three or four are not strong in high cards.

With seven or eight playing tricks, based on a long suit, the opener raises a barrage against the other side. If they double, the penalty will not be exorbitant. If they venture into the auction, it will have to be at the level of four or five.

Non-vulnerable, six tricks will suffice for a three bid. Something like:

1.  ♠ A J 10 x x x x          2.  ♠ A x x x x x x
    ♡ x x            or           ♡ —
    ◇ x                          ◇ Q J x x
    ♣ Q x x                      ♣ x x

while:

3.  ♠ K Q J 10 x x x      4.  ♠ Q J x x x x x x
    ♡ —                       ♡ x
    ◇ K Q J                  ◇ A K x
    ♣ x x x                  ♣ x

are both quite good enough for an opening four-spade bid, regardless of vulnerability.

**Responding to Three Bids.** To put up an opening three bid to game, partner need not have more than two of the suit. But he must have high cards – aces and kings – in the other suits. If he has a suit of his own, he will generally be wise to suppress it, for the chances are that he may run up against a singleton or void opposite.

Generally speaking, curb your enthusiasm when partner pre-empts. The time to get ideas is when you hear him open two of something, and that will come up for review in the next lesson.

CHART V – OPENER'S REBIDS ON HANDS OF 17–20 POINTS

| First round sequence | Rebid | | Determining factors |
|---|---|---|---|
| | 17–18 points | 19–20 points | |
| **One heart – one spade**<br><br>A response at the two level (two of a minor over a heart or spade) shows at least 9–10 points. Taking this into account, the opener's rebid with 18 is at the game level (as in 19–20 column) | Two no-trumps<br>or<br>three hearts<br>or<br>three spades<br>or<br>two clubs<br>or<br>diamonds | Three no-trumps<br>or<br>four hearts<br>or<br>four spades<br>or<br>three clubs<br>or<br>diamonds | A balanced hand (no singleton) with something in every suit.<br><br>A six- (or seven-) card suit of your own.<br><br>At least four cards in partner's suit.<br><br>Without the qualifications for any of the above, show a second (four-card suit), if you can. With 19 or more *jump* – to make certain that the bidding does not stop. |

## Exercises

You open one heart and partner responds one spade. What do you bid on:

1. ♠ K x
   ♡ A x x x x x
   ◇ Q x x
   ♣ K x

2. ♠ K x
   ♡ A x x x x
   ◇ A Q x
   ♣ K J x

3. ♠ Q x x x
   ♡ A K Q J x
   ◇ x x
   ♣ x x

4. ♠ x
   ♡ A J x x
   ◇ K J x x
   ♣ A J x x

5. ♠ A x
   ♡ A K Q x x x
   ◇ A x
   ♣ x x x

6. ♠ K Q x x
   ♡ A K x x x
   ◇ A J x x
   ♣ —

Your partner opens one spade, and over your two clubs, rebids two no-trumps. What do you say on:

7. ♠ x
   ♡ K J x
   ◇ x x x
   ♣ Q J 10 x x x

8. ♠ x x
   ♡ x x
   ◇ x x x
   ♣ A K J x x x

Your partner opens one diamond and rebids three no-trumps over your response of one heart. What do you say on:

9. ♠ x
   ♡ K x x x x x
   ◇ A x
   ♣ J x x x

10. ♠ x x
    ♡ A K Q x x
    ◇ x x x
    ♣ x x x

11. ♠ x x
    ♡ A K x x
    ◇ K x x x
    ♣ K Q x

Your partner opens one spade, and over your response of two clubs, rebids two hearts. What do you say on:

12. ♠ J x x
    ♡ K x x
    ◇ x x
    ♣ A J x x x

13. ♠ Q x x
    ♡ K x
    ◇ x x x
    ♣ A Q x x x

14. ♠ K x
    ♡ Q x
    ◇ J 10 9 x
    ♣ A J x x x

You deal and bid one spade on:

15. ♠ Q x x x x
    ♡ A J x
    ◇ x x
    ♣ K Q x

What do you bid if partner's response is: (*a*) Three spades? (*b*) Three diamonds? (*c*) Three clubs?

You bid one diamond and partner calls three hearts. What do you say on:

16. ♠ x x
    ♡ x
    ◇ A Q J 10 x x
    ♣ A J x x

At love all, what do you bid as dealer on:

17. ♠ K x
    ♡ x x
    ◇ A K Q J x x x
    ♣ x x

At love all, what do you bid as dealer on:

18. ♠ x
    ♡ K Q J 10 x x x
    ◇ x x x
    ♣ x x

Your partner opens three hearts. What do you call on:

19. ♠ x x
    ♡ A x x
    ◇ A x x x
    ♣ K x x x

Your partner opens one diamond. The next player passes. What do you call on:

20.  ♠ x x
     ♡ K J 10 x x x x
     ◇ x x
     ♣ x x

# LESSON VI

# BIDDING

**Two Bids.** The real art in bridge, of course, is to hold good cards, and in this lesson, we shall show the measure of our skill. Big hands are few and far between, but when they occur, it is important to make the most of them.

**Two Clubs.** When players cut each other for the first time, they usually enquire: 'What system shall we play?' It could be Precision or the Forcing Two, but in Britain it is almost invariably Two Clubs, usually the ACOL form of it. Occasionally a player picks up a rock-crusher – a hand strong enough to yield game on *its own*, even if partner holds a Yarborough (no honour card). A case in point would be something like:

♠ A K Q x x    ♡ A K Q x x    ◇ A    ♣ x x

A game should be there. But in what?

To find out needs a couple of rounds of bidding. Otherwise there is no guarantee that there will be even one round, for responder may have a blizzard, and then he will allow the hand to be passed out in one spade.

The opener ensures that the auction will be kept going *till game* by using a convention. If he has agreed with partner on the two clubs system, he opens proceedings with an *artificial* bid of two clubs.

**A Game Demand Bid.** Known as a game demand bid, this has nothing to do with clubs, or any other suit. It is simply a message to partner saying: 'Whatever you do, don't drop the bidding. I have a super hand, but I need a little *time* to show you the highlights, and then, with your help, to find the best contract.'

**Denial Bids.** On a worthless hand, responder calls two diamonds. That, again, is conventional and has no bearing on diamonds. The name for it in bridge parlance is a 'negative' or 'denial' bid, because it denies as much as an ace and a king or a king-queen and a king.

Try out the convention with the hand above.

| *Opener* | *Responder* |
|---|---|
| ♠ A K Q x x | ♠ x x x |
| ♡ A K Q x x | ♡ x |
| ♢ A | ♢ x x x x x |
| ♣ x x | ♣ x x x x |

### Bidding

| Two clubs | Two diamonds |
|---|---|
| Two spades | Two no-trumps |
| Three hearts | Three spades |
| Four spades | No bid |

The first round bids by both players are purely conventional.

Responder's two no-trumps – over two spades – is again conventional, denying even secondary values. He cannot pass below the game level, and two no-trumps is the accepted form of denial on the second round. With anything like a decent suit – K J x x x or Q J x x x x – responder would show it even at the

three level. Since his hand is utterly useless, he calls two
no-trumps – *conventionally*.

**Positive Responses.** On

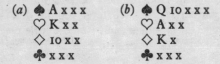

|       | (a) | ♠ A x x x | (b) | ♠ Q 10 x x x |
|-------|-----|-----------|-----|--------------|
|       |     | ♡ K x x   |     | ♡ A x x      |
|       |     | ♢ 10 x x  |     | ♢ K x        |
|       |     | ♣ x x x   |     | ♣ x x x      |

The response to a two-clubs opening on (a) is two no-
trumps. This is positive – showing not less than an ace and a
king. On the first round, *only* a two-diamond bid is a denial.

It is important not to confuse the first and second round
negative responses since that would make all the difference to
partner.

The response to a two-clubs opening with (b) is two
spades. That, again, is positive. A five-card suit, headed by
the queen, is worth showing and gives partner a better picture
than two no-trumps.

**Forcing Two Convention.** As you can see, game demand
bids are governed by accepted conventions. The opening and
the response show strength and weakness, not clubs or
diamonds.

Under the forcing two system, still popular in America, *any*
opening two call in a suit is a game demand bid. Instead of an
artificial call in clubs, the opener shows his longest suit on the
first round. And the negative response is two no-trumps.

Here is an illustration of the two conventions, applied alternatively to the same deal:

|  | |
|---|---|
| *Opener* | *Responder* |
| ♠ A K Q x x | ♠ x x |
| ♡ A K J x | ♡ x x x x |
| ◇ A K | ◇ x x x |
| ♣ x x | ♣ J x x x |

| *On the Two Clubs* | | *On the Forcing Two* | |
|---|---|---|---|
| *Opener* | *Responder* | *Opener* | *Responder* |
| Two clubs | Two diamonds | Two spades | Two no-trumps |
| Two spades | Two no-trumps | Three hearts | Four hearts |
| Three hearts | Four hearts | No bid | |
| No bid | | | |

**Showing a Fit.** Observe that as soon as hearts are mentioned, responder supports his partner, despite his miserable hand.

Having made a negative bid on the first round, responder should always show a fit for his partner's suit as soon as he can. Any *four* cards in the suit – or three cards headed by the ace, king or queen – constitute a fit.

It follows that the opener must not interpret a simple raise in his suit – after a denial bid on the first round – as showing any high cards at all. On the hand above, he passes four hearts.

**Near-Game Hands.** A player does not often pick up thirteen cards which can be expected to yield game all on their own, without any help from partner. That is why Game Demand bids are rare. A less uncommon occurrence is a *near*-Game hand – about eight playing tricks, based on a good, long suit. Something like:

| 1. ♠ A J x | 2. ♠ K x |
|---|---|
| ♡ A K Q x x x | ♡ A Q |
| ◇ x | ◇ A K J 10 x x x |
| ♣ K Q x | ♣ Q x |

On the Forcing Two system there is no way of announcing big

distributional hands on the first round. But the Two Clubs convention allows intermediate bids of two in the other three suits. Since only two clubs is forcing to game, it is possible to convey a *near*-game hand based on spades, hearts or diamonds.

On 1, the opening is two hearts, and on 2, it is two diamonds.

**Responding to Intermediate Two-bids.** Partner can pass if he has nothing. But he needs very little to keep open the auction – especially if he has anything at all in the opener's suit.

Under Acol – the best known of the Two-Clubs Systems – any opening Two-bid is unconditionally forcing for one round. Without as much as an ace and a king or a king and a K Q, responder calls *two no-trumps*. Thereafter he can pass, unless the opener takes drastic action – like a jump in a new suit.

Do not worry too much about systems at present. That can wait. Bear in mind that a Two-bid carries the promise of a good long suit and about eight playing tricks. Holding a blizzard in response, pass. But don't forget to put on a pair of rose-coloured glasses when you look at your hand.

The opening is two hearts and responder holds:

|  | (a) | (b) | (c) |
|---|---|---|---|
| ♠ | Q x x | x x | K Q x x x |
| ♡ | x x | J x x x | x |
| ◇ | A x x | A x x | x x x |
| ♣ | J x x x x | x x x x | A x x x |

What should he do? Knowing that partner has something like eight playing tricks of his own and a good suit, responder should:

on (a) call two no-trumps.

on (b) call three hearts.

A single raise in the opener's suit suggests an ace, but promises very little – just a fit in trumps. A double raise – four hearts here – would show good trumps, a fair hand, but no controls.

on (*c*) call two spades.

Unlike hands (*a*) and (*b*) there is enough here for a constructive response in a new suit.

Here is one more example: the opening is still two hearts and responder holds

$$(d) \quad \spadesuit \; K \, x \, x$$
$$\heartsuit \; x \, x$$
$$\diamondsuit \; A \, J \, x \, x$$
$$\clubsuit \; K \, x \, x \, x$$

The best response on it is *three* no-trumps – a jump.

As always, no-trump bids suggest a balanced hand, and the jump promises more strength than responder would need to keep open the bidding.

**Opening Two No-trumps.** All the game and near-game hands discussed above had one feature in common: distribution. In other words, they were unbalanced.

Powerful balanced hands present fewer problems. We have already examined some that add up to 19–20. The opener showed his strength by carrying his rebid to the game level on the second round.

With more, a *good* 20, with a 5-card suit perhaps, and up to 22, the usual practice is to open two no-trumps. Responder raises to three on 4 points. This is how it works:

|  | *Opener* | *Responder* |
|---|---|---|
| 1. | ♠ A J x | ♠ 10 x |
|  | ♡ K J x | ♡ x x x |
|  | ◇ A Q 10 x | ◇ J x x |
|  | ♣ A Q x | ♣ K x x x x |

2.   ♠ K x          ♠ 10 x x x
      ♡ A Q x        ♡ J x
      ◇ K x x        ◇ Q J x x x
      ♣ A K Q x x     ♣ J x

Both hands are bid in the same way: two no-trumps – three no-trumps.

**Game Demand Bids – Balanced.** Finally, we come to balanced hands that add up to more than 22. Since almost anything opposite will suffice for game, the opener cannot take the risk of calling two no-trumps. Partner could pass and a game might be missed.

With 23–24 points, open two clubs and rebid two no-trumps. This is *not* forcing – the sole exception over a two clubs opening. With 25 or more the rebid is three no-trumps.

Partner must rise to the occasion and on comparatively slender values, visualize a slam.

Since the opener promises not less than 23 – and maybe more – responder can count up to the slam-target figure of 34 on 10 points. If his hand is anything like balanced, he wastes no time. Six no-trumps is the bid.

And on

| *Opener* | *Responder* |
|---|---|
| ♠ A J x | ♠ Q 10 x x x x |
| ♡ A K Q x | ♡ x x |
| ◇ A K x | ◇ x x x |
| ♣ K x x | ♣ A J |

the sequence should be

| *Opener* | *Responder* |
|---|---|
| Two clubs | Two diamonds |
| Two no-trumps | *Six* spades |

Knowing that he will find a fit with partner, responder need have no fears about his trump suit. Q 10 x x x x may not look impressive – by itself. Opposite a balanced game hand, it is formidable. The two clubs opening announces game values. The no-trump rebid shows a balanced hand, and therefore, a certain guard in spades.

After a game demand bid, responder should show his imagination – and plenty of courage.

In the old days balanced game-giving hands with 25 points or more were opened three no-trumps. This is no longer so. The ACOL variant is now pretty nearly universal (except on One Club systems). Today an opening bid of three no-trumps tells a very different story, showing a long *solid* minor with nothing much outside, something like:

$$♠ \text{ 10 x } ♡ \text{ Q x x } ♢ \text{ J } ♣ \text{ A K Q J x x x}$$

Hand 17 in the Exercises after Lesson V would qualify.

**Blackwood.** Good bidding depends largely on common sense, not on conventions. Two-bids provide an exception. Slams give rise to another.

There are situations when the combined values point to a slam. Twelve tricks should be there. But much of the strength is distributional and it is just possible, that before you can get going, opponents will cash two aces.

Blackwood – the simplest of all bridge conventions – has been devised to guard against this danger. It consists of an artificial bid of *four no-trumps*, asking partner how many aces he has. The responses are, of course, equally artificial. Five clubs – the cheapest bid over four no-trumps – denies even one ace. Five diamonds shows one ace; five hearts, two aces; five spades, three aces. For every ace the *rank* of the suit is raised by one. With all four aces – a most unlikely event – the response would be five no-trumps.

Try out the convention with:

$$♠ \text{ K Q x } ♡ \text{ A K Q J x x } ♢ \text{ x x } ♣ \text{ x x}$$

Over your opening heart, responder forces – two spades. Then, over three hearts, he calls three spades.

You are clearly in the slam zone, and yet opponents may just have two aces. Partner would bid in the same way on

(a) ♠ A J 10 x x x  (b) ♠ A J x x x x x
    ♡ x            ♡ x x
    ♢ K Q J  or  ♢ A x
    ♣ K Q J       ♣ A Q

With (a) a small slam will go down. With (b) a grand slam is unbreakable. To find out the position, the opener calls *four no-trumps*. If partner shows one ace only, he stops in five spades. If he hears five hearts (two aces), the contract will be a small slam. And if responder can show all three missing aces, the final bid will be seven.

The purpose of Blackwood is not to reach slams, but to keep out of slam contracts that cannot be made.

Use the convention sparingly, bearing this proviso in mind: make sure *first* that you know in what suit the hand will be played. It can be your suit or partner's. And it can be no-trumps. But don't ask the Blackwood question until you know which it is to be.

**Finding the Kings.** An extension of the Blackwood convention provides for the location of missing kings. The procedure is the same as before, but it takes place at a higher level. Five no-trumps conveys the inquiry and six clubs denies one king.

Until you gain a good deal of experience, you will be wise to keep this part of Blackwood in cold storage. It is useful, but it will keep.

## Exercises

You are playing the two clubs convention. What do you open on:

| 1. ♠ K J x | 2. ♠ K J x | 3. ♠ A K |
|---|---|---|
| ♡ A Q x | ♡ K Q J x x x x | ♡ K Q x |
| ◇ A J x x | ◇ A Q | ◇ K Q 10 9 |
| ♣ A Q x | ♣ x | ♣ A Q J x |

Your partner opens two clubs. The next player passes. What do you bid on:

| 4. ♠ Q J 10 x x x x | 5. ♠ A 10 x x |
|---|---|
| ♡ x x | ♡ x x x |
| ◇ Q x | ◇ K J x |
| ♣ K x | ♣ J x x |

You are still playing the two clubs convention. Partner opens two spades and the next player passes. What do you bid on:

| 6. | 7. | 8. | 9. |
|---|---|---|---|
| ♠ K J x x | ♠ J x x | ♠ x x | ♠ 10 x |
| ♡ x x | ♡ x | ♡ J 10 x x | ♡ K x x |
| ◇ x x | ◇ A x x x x | ◇ Q x x | ◇ K J x x |
| ♣ K Q x x x | ♣ x x x x | ♣ Q J x x | ♣ K J x x |

You are playing the forcing two and your partner opens two hearts. The next player passes. What do you bid on:

| 10. ♠ x x x x | 11. ♠ A Q x |
|---|---|
| ♡ x x | ♡ x x x |
| ◇ — | ◇ K x x |
| ♣ x x x x x x x | ♣ J x x x |

The bidding:

| South | North |
|-------|-------|
| One heart | Four hearts |
| Four no-trumps | ? |

Sitting North, what do you bid on:

12. ♠ A Q x  
    ♡ Q 10 x x x  
    ◇ x  
    ♣ K J x x

13. ♠ x x  
    ♡ A x x x  
    ◇ A x x x  
    ♣ A J x

The bidding:

| South | North |
|-------|-------|
| One spade | Four spades |

Sitting South, what do you bid on:

14. ♠ A Q x x x  
    ♡ A K x x  
    ◇ K x  
    ♣ x x

15. ♠ K Q J x x  
    ♡ K x  
    ◇ K x  
    ♣ A Q J x

The bidding:

| South | North |
|-------|-------|
| Two no-trumps | Four no-trumps |

Sitting South, what do you bid on:

16. ♠ A Q x  
    ♡ K x x x  
    ◇ A Q x  
    ♣ A Q x

17. ♠ A Q x  
    ♡ K J x x  
    ◇ A Q 10  
    ♣ A Q 10

At love all, your partner opens three hearts. What do you bid on:

18. ♠ A K x          19. ♠ x
    ♡ x x                 ♡ K x x
    ◇ A K Q x             ◇ A K Q J x x
    ♣ K x x x             ♣ A x x

         20. ♠ A K Q 10 x x x
             ♡ A x x
             ◇ x
             ♣ A x

## LESSON VII

# BIDDING

**Defensive Bids.** For the rest of this lesson we shall sit E W, on the defenders' side of the usual diagram. South will open the bidding, and it will fall to us to pass, stoically, or to enter the auction, according to our values.

**The Overcall.** To intervene defensively – to overcall or 'butt-in', in bridge terminology – requires rather less high card strength than it does to open. But the suit itself must be more substantial. If the defender commits himself to a short or flimsy trump suit, he may run into a nasty double from North. Sitting between the opener and his partner, West may find himself caught in a pincer movement. And if his trumps are shaky, it may be expensive.

Over any suit opening, overcall one spade on:

1. ♠ K Q J x x    2. ♠ Q J 10 x x x
   ♡ K Q x    or    ♡ A x x
   ◇ x x            ◇ K x x
   ♣ x x x          ♣ x

But if your suit is not spades, and you must bid at the two level, the first hand does not quite make the grade.

Vulnerability is an important factor. Look at the table of penalties in Lesson I and you will see how costly it is to go down vulnerable, especially when opponents double.

**Fewer Points, Better Trumps.** Hand 2 is just about a minimum butt-in at the two level vulnerable.

Take a look at these two hands:

(a) ♠ A x x     (b) ♠ K Q J 10 9 x
    ♡ x x x         ♡ x x
    ♢ A x x         ♢ K x x
    ♣ A J x x      ♣ x x

On (a) you open the bidding – but you do not contemplate butting-in. On (b) you butt-in – but you do not open. Yet the first example adds up to 13 and the second one to no more than 11, including distribution.

The lack of a decent trump suit in (a) and the solidity of the spades in (b) explain the paradox.

The opener approaches with a view to finding a fit. The defender has less time to explore and must be prepared to play the hand in the suit he calls.

**Partner's Response to Overcalls.** Partner does not keep the auction going for an overcall on a mere 6 points, as he would do for an opening. He can pass on 8–9, particularly if he fears a misfit. But he can support freely on three prospective trumps, for he expects the overcall to be based on a fair *five*-card suit. And once the fit is assured, he raises without undue inhibitions.

South opens one club and West calls one heart. North passes.

**East holds:**

1.  ♠ x x
    ♡ 10 x x
    ◇ A Q J x x
    ♣ K Q x

2.  ♠ A x
    ♡ J x x
    ◇ K Q x x
    ♣ A J x x

On 1, he raises to three, and on 2, to four. In short, he needs 1–2 points more to raise an overcall than an opening bid.

**Jump Overcalls.** Sometimes, a defender holds both a good suit and high cards outside. How should he convey the good news to his partner? The answer is: a *jump* overcall – one more than is necessary:

South opens one diamond. West has:

(a)  ♠ A K J 10 x x
     ♡ A K x
     ◇ x
     ♣ Q x x

or

(b)  ♠ K x
     ♡ A x
     ◇ x x
     ♣ A K Q J x x x

The bid is *two* spades on (a) and *three* clubs on (b).

**Single or Double Jumps.** Note that each time it is a *single* jump. A bid of three spades on (a) would convey a very different message to East. It would show something like:

♠ K Q J x x x x   ♡ x   ◇ x x   ♣ Q J x

A single jump overcall proclaims a powerful hand, based on a good suit – usually a six-card suit. A *double* jump, as above, is pre-emptive. It is an effort to shut out the other side and has little high card strength, though rarely less than seven cards in the suit bid. We have already come across this principle in Lesson V, when we examined pre-emptive bids by opener and responder. The idea is the same in defensive bidding.

**The Informatory Double.** A convention in universal use for purposes of defensive bidding is the artificial double of the opening call. The double asks partner to show his longest suit.

It often happens that West – sitting over South, the opener – has a useful hand, but there is no suit to which he cares to commit himself. The idea of the informatory or *take out* double, as it is known, is to enlist partner's help in finding a fit.

South calls one spade and West holds:

| 1. ♠ x | 2. ♠ x x | 3. ♠ A x |
|---|---|---|
| ♡ K J x x | ♡ A Q J x | ♡ Q 10 x x |
| ♢ A Q x x | ♢ K Q x x | ♢ A J x |
| ♣ K 10 x x | ♣ A Q x | ♣ K J x x |

If West picks a suit himself, he may easily find partner with a singleton or a doubleton. And yet there may well be – there probably is – an excellent fit in some other suit. To convey this picture to East, West doubles.

**When a Double is Conventional.** The double of a suit at the one level is always conventional, *unless* partner has made a bid. If he has, then it is an ordinary penalty double. But if he has not yet spoken or if he has passed, the double is informatory – for a take out.

Either defender can make an informatory double. And partner *must* respond. He cannot pass – just because he does not fancy his hand or because he is feeling depressed in general. There *is* an occasion for passing, but of that more later.

**Qualifications for a Double.** Knowing that partner will be put in that position, the doubler must not abuse the convention. He must have enough to stand *any* suit response – even if the hand opposite is trickless. That means shape, as well as high cards. Shortage in the opener's suit is always an asset since it guarantees a fit for any of the other suits which partner may bid.

The ideal pattern for an Informatory Double is 5–4–4–0 and the next best is 4–4–4–1. With either distribution, it is enough to have twelve high card points and that, too, may be shaded on occasion. Less shapely hands need a little more.

**Responder's Role.** The corollary to the above is that the responder to a double must take drastic action with as much as *ten points*. And this is the reasoning: even with nothing responder has to find a bid. Since ten points is a great deal more than nothing something special must be done about it. The answer is: *jump*. Make your bid, not at the lowest level, but at one higher.

This is how it works:

South opens one heart.

&spades; A J x x
&hearts; x x
&diamonds; K Q x
&clubs; K Q x x

&spades; K Q x x x
&hearts; x x
&diamonds; A x x x
&clubs; x x

Bidding:

| *South* | *West* | *North* | *East* |
|---|---|---|---|
| One heart | Double | No bid | *Two* spades |
| No bid | Three spades | No bid | Four spades |

**Bidding Sequence in Defence.** This sequence is worth a brief analysis.

1. West doubles – an informatory double, since partner has not bid – because he is good enough to enter the auction, but has only short suits himself.

He wants to hear partner's suit.

2. East *jumps*, because he would have had to say one spade on a blizzard. West could not expect from him more than 4–5 points – certainly not 10. He must show that he is a good deal better than he might be.

3. West raises to three, not four, because he has only a little over a minimum for an informatory double.

4. East can pass – if he likes. He is no longer forced to bid as he was on the first round. But he is too good to stop, particularly as the suit is spades, offering prospects of game at the four level.

**A Penalty Pass.** Responding to an informatory double is fairly simple, so long as you try to visualize the sort of hand opposite – some high cards, a balanced pattern, and probably a singleton or doubleton in the suit bid by opponents. You do not pass on a poor hand, because if you did, it would mean that the other side would need only seven tricks for the contract, with their chosen suit as trumps. They might easily make more, charging you 100 a time – 200 vulnerable – for overtricks. Far better for you to bid a suit on four 'rags', even if it means going down a trick or two.

The time to pass partner's take out double is when it *suits you* – when you have strength and length in the suit bid by opponents.

South calls one heart, your partner, West, doubles and North passes. You hold:

(1) ♠ x x x x    (2) ♠ x
    ♡ x x          ♡ Q J 10 9 x x
    ♢ Q x x x     ♢ J x x
    ♣ x x x       ♣ Q x x

On (1) you call a spade. Partner, remember, is prepared for spades and in response to a double, any suit is biddable. Your diamonds are slightly better, but you choose the cheapest bid – *one* spade rather than *two* diamonds.

On (2) you pass, because you *want* the hand to be played in one heart doubled. You expect opponents to go down, which is why the bid is known as a Penalty Pass.

**Double of One No-trump.** An entirely different situation presents itself when partner doubles one no-trump. He cannot have a shortage in opponents' suit, since they have not bid one. Therefore, it implies greater high card strength than in the case of an ordinary take out double. So if you have any high cards yourself, 6–7 points perhaps, the balance of strength is on your side and opponents are unlikely to make most of the tricks – seven out of thirteen. In short, you can expect a penalty. For that reason, the double of one no-trump – unlike the double of one of a suit – is known as a Business Double. It does not ask for partner's longest suit.

Of course, responder may have a feeble five or six-card suit and nothing else. Then he takes out the double. But with a completely balanced hand, almost any pretext is good enough to *stand* it – to pass in the hope of defeating the one no-trump contract.

When in doubt about the correct response, endeavour to picture partner's hand. That will give you most of the clues you need. And that, broadly speaking, is true of almost every situation at the bridge table.

**A Cue Bid.** It happens on occasion, that South can open the bidding, but that West or East has a huge hand – something approaching an opening two-club bid. If it is too strong for an informatory double or for a jump overcall, a player can make a *cue bid* in opponents' suit. Over one heart from an opponent, he calls two hearts! This is a game demand bid, like an opening two clubs, but it is made after the *other side* has opened the bidding.

South deals and calls one diamond.

West holds:

1. ♠ A Q J x      2. ♠ A K 10 x x
   ♡ A K Q x  or   ♡ A Q J x
   ◇ —             ◇ x
   ♣ A Q J 10 x    ♣ A Q J

He calls two *diamonds* and partner responds by showing his longest suit. So far, the procedure looks the same as in the case of an informatory double, but there is a vital difference. A cue bid keeps the bidding open till game is reached. Responder cannot pass, even on the second round, if partner's last call is below game level.

It is as well to be familiar with this convention, as it is widely known, and you may come across it when you meet experienced players. Until you have played bridge for quite a bit, however, you will be wise to leave it alone yourself. Like other specialized conventions, it is a useful gadget, but not one of the essentials.

**Sacrifice Bidding.** One of the greatest arts in defensive bidding lies in knowing when to sacrifice and when to double.

Apart from the informatory double, which arises only in clearly defined situations – at a *low level* and when partner has *not bid* – all doubles are known as business doubles.

When you think that opponents will fail in their contract, you double them to increase the penalty – to raise the stakes, as it were, on a particular hand.

A sacrifice – or 'save' – is a piece of spoiling tactics. You prefer to go down yourselves sooner than allow opponents to make their contract.

At equal vulnerability it is worth going two down doubled to save a game by opponents. But that is the maximum.

If you are vulnerable and the others are not, one down is all you can afford.

And to dispute a part score, one down *non*-vulnerable should be the limit.

The side which sacrifices must expect to be doubled – though it does not happen every time. When the bidding is highly competitive, when both sides strive hard to secure the contract, it is not always immediately apparent when one side oversteps the mark.

How, then, should you know when to double? There can be no fixed rules – only one or two guiding principles.

**The Time to Double for Penalties.** First, apply the technique you learned as responder in all these lessons. Add up the hands. Partner shows so much, you have so much more. That gives you a certain share of the pack. Can opponents make their contract with what is left? That approach gives you a line to the high card strength.

Next comes distribution. Your *long* suits won't take many tricks against a suit contract by opponents. Only the aces and kings are likely to be worth their points; and then not always, for they may be ruffed.

Finally, we come to the trump position. It is obvious that the more trumps you have the stronger you will be defensively. But here is something which is not so obvious: the Q 10 x x in trumps may be much better value than A x, when you contemplate doubling, say, a four-heart contract. Opponents *know* that they are without the ace of trumps and they are clearly prepared to lose that particular trick. But they can't know that you sit with the Q 10 x x and it may come to them as an unpleasant surprise.

**Luck.** This brings us to the important element of luck.

Many contracts are broken simply because declarer is unluckly, and that, of course, is the time to double. It happens this way: The trumps are spades. In the bidding declarer has shown a good trump suit. You sit *under* him with K J x. That is no good, because you may not make a trick at all. Your honours are 'finessible'. But if you sit *over* him, you will probably make both the king and the knave.

The first time, luck is with declarer. The second time, it is on your side.

Or the same position arises in a side suit bid by dummy. You sit *over* dummy with A Q 10.

You know, and declarer does not, that on this deal Fortune is with you.

If that is the distribution, and if it looks as if opponents have nothing to spare in high cards, you step in with a sharp double.

This is, no doubt, a more advanced form of bidding, but on the last lap we need not be backward.

**A Snap Double.** For the last example of all, we choose a low level contract, precisely because inexperienced players so often miss what are called 'snap doubles' – penalty doubles on the *first* round of bidding.

It needs no great imagination to double the enemy in a high contract which you expect to defeat by brute strength. Skill comes into its own, when partner opens, an opponent makes an overcall and you happen to hold the *right* cards.

Knowing that partner has enough to open the bidding, you don't require too much: four of the suit, headed by Q 10 x x or better; a couple of high cards, say, an ace and a king; and a shortage in partner's suit. That will generally yield six, seven, and even eight tricks in defence.

The fewer cards you have in partner's suit, the greater your strength in defence.

Partner opens one spade. The next man butts-in with two diamonds. You hold:

$$(a)\ \spadesuit\ x \qquad\qquad (b)\ \spadesuit\ A\,K\,X$$
$$\heartsuit\,K\,J\,x\,x \quad or \quad \heartsuit\,x\,x$$
$$\diamondsuit\,Q\,10\,x\,x \qquad\quad \diamondsuit\,A\,K\,x$$
$$\clubsuit\,K\,10\,x\,x \qquad\quad \clubsuit\,Q\,x\,x\,x\,x$$

Double on (a), but not on (b).

Only an experienced player will accept this paradox without raising at least two eyebrows. For, of course, (b) is a much better hand than (a). It is an interesting situation and one that occurs not infrequently. So let us look into it more closely.

On hand (b) you should be able to make a game easily; possibly a slam. If you double and set opponents two or three tricks, you will get little for your pains. It will turn out to be a sacrifice on their part – cheap or not quite so cheap. But that is all.

Turn to (a). Your own future is nebulous. You hate partner's spades, and no good contract – certainly no game contract – suggests itself. It may well be that your two hands don't fit anywhere and that you will go down in whatever contract you reach.

This time, moreover, your Q 10 x x in opponents' trump suit will spring a surprise. The two diamond caller may have started with A K J x x, hoping to make four tricks – perhaps all five. On account of the distribution, he can make no more than three. And if you add up the points, you will see that your side is pretty certain to hold the balance.

Definitely, _luck_ will be on your side – if you decide to double.

The technique in bridge – and it is less difficult than it may appear to you at this stage – is to enrol luck as an ally.

## Exercises

The opponent on your right opens one heart. What do you bid on:

1. ♠ A x x x
   ♡ x x
   ◇ K Q x x
   ♣ A K x

2. ♠ x
   ♡ A K J x
   ◇ Q J x x
   ♣ K x x x

3. ♠ K Q J 10 x x
   ♡ x
   ◇ A J x x
   ♣ K x

4. ♠ K Q 10 9 x
   ♡ x x
   ◇ A J x x
   ♣ x x

5. ♠ K Q 10 9 x x x
   ♡ x
   ◇ Q J 10
   ♣ x x

6. ♠ x x
   ♡ x
   ◇ A K Q J x x x
   ♣ A x x

North, your partner, bids one heart. East calls one spade. Sitting South, what do you bid on:

7. ♠ K J 10 9 x
   ♡ x
   ◇ K x x
   ♣ Q J x x

8. ♠ K J x
   ♡ 10 x x
   ◇ K x x
   ♣ A 10 x x

9. ♠ A Q x
   ♡ x x
   ◇ 10 x x x
   ♣ K x x

10. ♠ K x x x x
    ♡ K Q x x x
    ◇ —
    ♣ K J x

11. ♠ J 10 9 x x x
    ♡ x x
    ◇ Q x x
    ♣ x x

12. ♠ A x x
    ♡ 10 x x
    ◇ A Q x x
    ♣ K x x

North calls one club. East, your partner, doubles and South passes. Sitting West, what do you bid on:

13. ♠ x
    ♡ K x x x x
    ◇ A K x x
    ♣ x x x

14. ♠ x x x
    ♡ Q x x
    ◇ x x
    ♣ K Q J 10 x

15. ♠ Q x x
    ♡ 10 x x
    ◇ J x x x
    ♣ K Q 10

16. ♠ K J 10 x x x
    ♡ A 10 x
    ◇ Q x
    ♣ x x

17. ♠ 10 x
    ♡ J x x
    ◇ K Q J x x
    ♣ A J x

18. ♠ x x x x
    ♡ K Q J
    ◇ x x
    ♣ x x x x

Your side only is vulnerable. Sitting South, you open one diamond, West calls one spade, North two diamonds and East four spades. What do you bid on:

19. ♠ A Q
    ♡ x x
    ◇ A K Q x x x
    ♣ K x x

20. ♠ x x
    ♡ K Q x
    ◇ A 10 x x
    ♣ A K x x

# *Part Three*

## LESSON VIII

## CARD PLAY

**Suit Establishment.** The best player in the world can only make one trick with an ace. The others have to be developed. A king-queen combination will yield a trick – but only after the ace has been driven out. Similarly, the Q J 10 will score in time – after the ace and king have left the field.

And so it goes on. Every card has its day – in strict order of seniority.

With honour sequences, as above, declarer develops tricks by forcing out still higher honours. By leading the king from K Q he either wins a trick or concedes it to the ace; and then the queen is good.

**The Deuce Becomes a Winner.** And what of the little x's – the deuce, for instance?

The same principle applies. Since the deuce is the lowest of the low, it becomes established only when opponents have no card left in its particular suit. The longer the suit, the easier it is for declarer to turn the deuce into a winner.

For it is a case of driving out the higher cards, and the fewer there are in enemy hands, the sooner will the deuce come into its own.

The corollary is that in a short suit the x's cannot be set up at all. If one of the opponents has as many cards as you have, he will always retain one to beat the lowly deuce.

Compare these holdings:

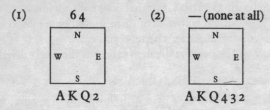

(1)        6 4        (2)        — (none at all)

A K Q 2        A K Q 4 3 2

Each time seven cards are out against you, which means that one of the defenders must have four at least. You can establish one or two of your small cards in (2), because you are *longer* than either West or East. Only a very unlucky 6–1 break of the outstanding cards can stop you. But no amount of luck can help you in (1). That deuce just is not *long* enough.

Add two x's to dummy's holding and at once the deuce's prospects take on a rosy hue.

7 6 4 3

A K Q 2

You see the difference? With only five cards out the chances are that neither opponent will have more than three – *three* to your *four*.

This is the sort of holding which declarer often seeks to develop:

A K 4 3 2 opposite 7 6 5 in dummy.

Opponents are left with five of the suit between them. They happen to be the Q J 10 9 8, but that does not really matter.

What is important is that *all* of them should be removed, for only then will the smaller x's become masters.

The suit will not always break evenly, but the likely division of the five cards is 3–2.

**Exhausting Opponents.** The ace, followed by the king, will denude one of the defenders altogether. The other will have one card left.

To remove it from the scene of action, declarer leads a third round. That trick is lost. But now both opponents have been exhausted of the suit. The three-spot and the deuce have been set up. They are masters.

Try it with a combined holding of ten cards, deal yourself:

A 10 x x x x x opposite x x x in dummy.

Defenders are left with the K Q J, and unless one of them has all three and his partner none, the whole suit can be set up in *two* rounds. The ace brings down the queen and the knave. A trick is conceded to the king. And the whole suit is good. Result: six winners and one loser.

In setting up his long suit, declarer subtracts from thirteen the number of cards he and dummy have between them. The difference is the number held by opponents. This tells declarer how often the suit must be led – assuming a likely division of the outstanding cards. All that is left is to count them as they fall, as a check against a bad break – or bad arithmetic.

**Counting the Cards.** Counting in bridge is all-important, and yet you need hardly give it a thought. After a while you will find that it is just 'doing what comes naturally'. It goes like this: Two rounds and all follow: eight cards gone. Third round and East shows out: eleven gone, and there are no more in dummy. I have one left, so West must have the other. And if mine is the four or the five, I am pretty certain that it is a loser. West would not have played his higher cards to keep the deuce or the three.

**On Blocking.** Suit establishment in itself presents no problem at all. Where care is needed sometimes is in handling the entries – in looking after communications between the two hands.

The simplest case is the manipulation of a suit which needs no establishing at all. With four cards left, the position is:

♠ A 2
♡ 2
♢ 2
♣ —

♠ K Q J 3
♡ —
♢ —
♣ —

Of course, declarer can make all four spade tricks – but only if he leads them out in the right order. Should he fail to play the ace on the *first* round, the suit will be *blocked*. Try *not* playing the ace first. As you see, the second trick is taken in dummy and there is no way back.

When holdings in the same suit are unequal in length, play the top card from the *shorter* holding first.

West opens a spade against three no-trumps.

    ♠ x x x
    ♡ A K x
    ♢ A K x
    ♣ A x x x

    ♠ A J
    ♡ x x x
    ♢ Q J 10 x x
    ♣ x x x

South takes East's Queen with the ace and . . .?

Yes, a *small* diamond to the ace, then the king and back to the South hand with dummy's little diamond – the vital link.

If declarer, thoughtlessly, leads a high diamond first and parts with dummy's x, the way back will be blocked by the A K.

When a set-up suit – one in which there are no losers – is unevenly divided between the two hands, be careful to keep communications open with the *longer* holding.

**Communications with Dummy.** Most of the time, of course, your winners will not be presented to you all ready on a plate. You will have to set them up yourself, and again you will need to nurse your entries or the tricks will slip through your fingers – after you have set them up.

We are in three no-trumps and West leads a club.

| Declarer | Dummy |
|----------|-------|
| ♠ J 10 9 8 | ♠ x x x |
| ♡ A x x | ♡ K Q x |
| ◇ x x x | ◇ A K x x |
| ♣ x x x | ♣ A K Q |

Don't play anything yet. *Always* size up the prospects before touching a card.

Dummy has all suits well guarded, so there is no apparent danger that opponents can grab five tricks quickly, before we get going. Time is on our side.

How many winners have we? Three in hearts, two in diamonds and three more in clubs. That gives us eight and we need one more for our contract.

That spade combination should provide the ninth trick. The knave being the fourth highest in rank, it will need three rounds to drive out his seniors – the ace, king, and queen. And that presents no difficulty, for dummy has three spades, and the suit can be played from either hand.

**Carelessness.** Yet there is still room for a mistake – or shall we say, for carelessness.

As they come in with their top spades, opponents may switch to hearts. It does not matter if they do, of course, for declarer can stop hearts three times. But it makes all the difference *where* he takes the first trick – his own hand or dummy.

Can you see why? After that fourth spade has been set up, declarer will have to *get back* to his hand to cash it. How? The heart ace is the only entry. If it is used prematurely, that spade – the ninth, decisive trick – can be written off. That is why, if the enemy switches to hearts, the first two heart tricks must be won on the table.

Look after the entries, the communications – especially

when you are setting up a long x in a hand which is weak in high cards.

**Ducking.** Let us get back to our first example and examine it in a setting of twenty-six cards.

A spade is led against three no-trumps.

| Declarer | Dummy |
|----------|-------|
| ♠ A K x | ♠ x x x |
| ♡ A K x x | ♡ x x |
| ♢ A Q x | ♢ x x x |
| ♣ x x x | ♣ A K x x x |

Count. There is no immediate danger, no gap anywhere in our defences. What of the attack? Five tricks are ready-made in the closed hand. To make the contract, dummy must provide four more. So we turn to the clubs.

Five clubs are out. Barring accidents, one opponent will hold three and the other two. That means that the club x's will not be established till three rounds have been played.

Any trouble? Yes. If declarer leads the ace, the king and a small one, he will make the last two x's good, but he will be unable to get at them. For dummy has no entry, outside the clubs themselves.

To solve his problem of communications, declarer ducks – he plays a *small* club from dummy first. Opponents win the trick, needless to say. They are bound to make one club anyway.

But no matter what suit is returned, declarer wins and leads out the ace and king of clubs. The last (third) round clears the suit and declarer *remains in dummy* to cash his two winners.

**Ducking Costs Nothing.** Ducking – playing low from a holding headed by high cards – is designed to *use up* one round of the suit. That helps to denude the defenders, each of whom will have one card fewer left in that suit. It costs nothing, for it only means conceding a trick sooner, rather than later.

**Ducking Twice.** The contract is three no-trumps, but try to make five (eleven tricks) on this hand:

|   | Declarer |   | Dummy |
|---|----------|---|-------|
| ♠ | A K J    | ♠ | x x x |
| ♡ | A K Q    | ♡ | x x x |
| ◇ | A K Q x  | ◇ | x x |
| ♣ | x x x    | ♣ | A x x x x |

Apply the same technique as in the previous example. Try working it out by yourself, assuming, as before, that the outstanding clubs break reasonably.

Got it?

Exactly. Duck *twice*. Play a small club from dummy. Then, on winning the next trick, another small club. That does it, for now the *last* club in enemy hands will fall on the ace and the lead will be in dummy – where you want it – at the *right moment*.

Again, it is a case of preserving the entry till you are ready to use it – till the suit is established.

**The Case for the Defence.** Now we move over to the E W seats. For at bridge, half the time we hunt with the hounds and the other half we run with the hare.

South, the declarer, tries to make his contract. East and West, the defenders, endeavour to break it. What is good for South is bad for E W, and vice versa. That applies in every situation. When South seeks to establish a suit, East and West plan to thwart him.

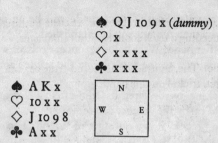

♠ Q J 10 9 x (*dummy*)
♡ x
◇ x x x x
♣ x x x

♠ A K x
♡ 10 x x
◇ J 10 9 8
♣ A x x

You are West, and against South's three no-trumps, you open the knave of diamonds.

We shall have a lot more to say about opening leads later. But it is never too soon to note that defenders, like declarer, try to set up winners – to establish the smaller cards. That is why the opening lead against no-trump contracts is made from length and not from strength. The longer the suit, the more x's you may eventually establish.

Now let us get back to that knave of diamonds. Partner, East, plays the deuce. South wins with the queen and leads a small spade.

West, let us say, goes up with the king and leads another diamond to the third trick. East follows. South takes it with the king and plays a second spade.

**The Hold Up.** What should West do?

The beginner will go up with his ace automatically, because it is the natural thing to do. He can take a trick, so why lose it?

The more experienced player will duck. He will hold up his ace – to kill dummy's long spades.

**Timing.** Declarer has no possible access to the table apart from the spades themselves. But he may well have three spades. If that is the case, and the ace and king are used up on the first two rounds, South's *third* spade will be an entry to dummy. And by then the suit will be established.

If, on the other hand, West holds up once, declarer will only be able to cross over to the table *before* the spades are established – and never again.

Just as ducking by declarer has the effect of creating an entry, so a hold up by the defence can remove it.

To be more precise, it is a question of timing. The ace will win one trick anyway. But it makes all the difference whether it wins *before* or *after* the suit has been set up.

**Putting Theory into Practice.** If you are not absolutely clear about it, try both ways. Play the ace and king on the first two rounds of the suit. You will find that South will then have access to dummy and will make *three* spade tricks in all. Next, hold up once. It will make no difference whether you do it on the first or the second round. The result will be – as you will see by playing out the cards – that South will be confined to *one* spade trick only.

**Killing an Entry.** Alter dummy's holding by one card. Give it a certain entry outside spades.

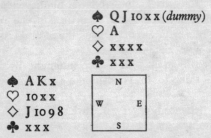

♠ Q J 10 x x (*dummy*)
♡ A
♢ x x x x
♣ x x x

♠ A K x
♡ 10 x x
♢ J 10 9 8
♣ x x x

West knows exactly what to do. He holds up once. But what should he lead when he comes in the first time?

You are quite right. It must be a heart. The vital entry to the spades must be removed while there is time – *before* the suit has been established.

And if dummy's heart holding were A x, the switch to hearts would still be imperative. West would then hope that his partner had the king to kill that entry.

**Yet Another Hold Up.** Modify the hand once more, and this time let us deal the whole pack.

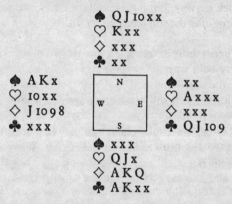

Go through the motions as before. West plays well in holding up once in spades. Every time he comes in, he returns a diamond. With six cards out of the way, the position is:

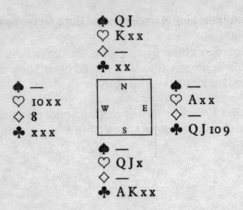

**Spotlight on East.** South leads the queen of hearts, and the spotlight turns on East.

Again, the beginner's fingers itch to play that ace. And that would be very helpful – to South, the enemy. Why? Because once the ace is out of the way, the master card in hearts will be the king, and the king is in dummy – with the two spade winners.

It is East's turn to hold up. And if declarer leads the knave, East must hold up again – for the same reason as before.

Play that hand over again, preferably from South's angle. Now how simple it is to make nine tricks if West or East slips up. But observe also how hopeless the contract becomes if the defenders cooperate in barring declarer's access to dummy.

**Hold Up by Declarer.** For the last example of the lesson we resume declarer's privileged positon in the South seat.

West leads the king of spades against three no-trumps.

♠ x x
♡ A x x
◇ K Q J 10 x
♣ x x x

♠ A x x
♡ K x x
◇ x x x
♣ A K x x

The count reveals no difficulty, at first sight. Nine tricks are available in: the ace of spades; the ace and king of hearts; four diamonds; and the ace and king of clubs.

The diamonds need little in the way of establishing – just one round to drive out the ace. And there is no entry problem.

**Winners and Losers.** South has the winners, but his danger is that he may not make them in time. If things go wrong, the defence may collect five tricks *before* declarer makes his nine.

East or West can easily have five spades. Once the ace has gone, four of those spades can take tricks. And then there is the ace of diamonds.

Can South do anything about it? Not if five spades and the ace of diamonds are held by the *same* defender. But there is no reason why they should be. And if they are divided South need not worry.

Do you see the solution? If not, have a look at all four hands, as they might well be in reality –

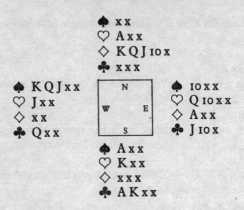

Does that give you any ideas?

If South wins the first spade trick – or the second – East will still have a spade to return when he comes in with the ace of diamonds. But if South holds up his ace till the *third* round, East will be denuded of spades.

**Cutting the East-West Road.** Once more it is a problem of communications. When we sat E W we tried to deny declarer an entry to his long suit in dummy. Now the roles are reversed. Sitting South, we try to stop the traffic between East and West.

Situations of this type arise again and again – especially in no-trump contracts. Each side seeks to develop its long suit – to set up the small cards. And each side nurses its entries and attacks the enemy's. For it is not much good having winners if you cannot get at them.

## Exercises

1. ♠ x x x x
   ♡ K x x
   ◇ x x x x
   ♣ A K

   ```
        N
    W       E
        S
   ```

   ♠ A K x
   ♡ A x x
   ◇ x x x x
   ♣ J x x

   You are South, declarer, at a contract of one no-trump.

   West leads the deuce of spades and your king takes East's knave.

   What card do you lead to the second trick?

2. ♠ Q J 10
   ♡ x x x x
   ◇ A K x
   ♣ K x x

   ```
        N
    W       E
        S
   ```

   ♠ x x x
   ♡ A K x
   ◇ Q x x
   ♣ A x x x

   The contract is two no-trumps.

   West leads a small diamond which you win in dummy with the king.

   What card do you play to the second trick?

3. ♠ x x
   ♡ K x x
   ◇ Q J x x
   ♣ K Q J 10

The contract is three no-trumps.

West leads a small spade. East goes up with the ace and returns the queen of spades.

   ♠ K 10 x
   ♡ A x x
   ◇ A K x x
   ♣ x x x

What card should South play?

4. ♠ x x
   ♡ x x
   ◇ K J x x x x
   ♣ K x x

The contract is three no-trumps.

West leads a small spade. East goes up with the queen.

   ♠ A x x
   ♡ Q x x
   ◇ A Q x
   ♣ A x x x

What card should South play?

5. ♠ K x x x x
   ♡ x x x
   ◇ x x
   ♣ 10 x x

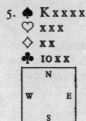

♠ A x x
♡ A K x
◇ A K x
♣ J x x x

The contract is two no-trumps.

West leads a heart, which South wins with the king. The second trick is taken in the closed hand with the ace of spades.

What card should South play from his own hand, and from dummy, to the third trick?

6. ♠ x x x
   ♡ A Q x x
   ◇ x x
   ♣ A x x x

♠ K Q J
♡ K J x
◇ A K x x x
♣ x x

West leads the king of clubs against three no-trumps by South. What card should declarer play from dummy to the first trick, and why?

7. ♠ J x x
    ♡ A
    ◇ A K x x x x     West leads a heart against six no-
    ♣ x x x     trumps by South. Which card should

declarer lead from dummy to the
second trick?

    ♠ A K x
    ♡ K x x x
    ◇ x x
    ♣ A K Q x

8.         ♠ x x x
           ♡ A
           ◇ x x x
           ♣ Q J 10 x x x

    ♠ Q J 10 9 x
    ♡ x x x x
    ◇ x x
    ♣ A K

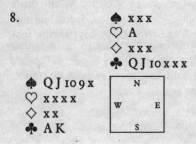

Sitting West, you lead the queen of
spades against three no-trumps by
South. Declarer wins and leads a
club. What card should you lead to
the third trick?

9. ♠ x x x
   ♡ x x
   ◇ A x
   ♣ A Q 10 9 x x

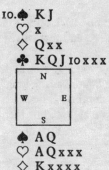

   ♠ x x
   ♡ x x x
   ◇ K Q x x
   ♣ K J x x

West opens the queen of spades against three no-trumps by South. Declarer wins in his hand and finesses the queen of clubs. What card should East return after taking the second trick with the king of clubs?

10. ♠ K J
    ♡ x
    ◇ Q x x
    ♣ K Q J 10 x x x

West leads a small spade against three no-trumps by South. What cards should declarer play, from his own hand and from dummy, to the first trick?

    ♠ A Q
    ♡ A Q x x x
    ◇ K x x x
    ♣ x

# LESSON IX

# CARD PLAY

**Finessing.** The purpose of a finesse is to take advantage of a 50–50 chance – to make an A Q do the work, sometimes, of an A K.

The basis of a finesse is hope – the hope that a missing card is where you want it to be.

The occasion to finesse is when you hold – in your own hand or in dummy – an honour sequence from which a card in the middle is missing.

This is known as a Tenace.

Finally, the technique of a finesse consists in playing *through* the missing card up to the tenace.

This is how it works:

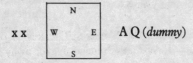

By laying down the ace first, you make one trick only. On the second round the Q will fall to a hostile K, and that will be that.

But by leading from West *up to* the A Q you *may* win both tricks. It will depend on whether North or South has the king. The point is that North plays first, *before* dummy. If he holds the king, he is helpless. He will doubtless play low, but then dummy's queen will take the trick. And if he goes up with the king, it will be headed by the ace.

**A Chance to Nothing.** Since the king – or any other given card – is as likely to be with North as with South, the finesse will succeed half the time. And it will be all profit. For the alternative, leading out the ace tamely, cannot gain at all in the ordinary way.

Here is another typical finesse position:

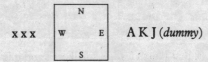

By leading the ace, followed by the king, you cannot expect to make more than two tricks. But if North has the queen, you can play *through* her, landing all three tricks.

All West does is to play from his hand, waiting for North's

card. If it is a low one, the knave is played from dummy. If it is the queen, West naturally wins with the ace or king.

Half the time, the missing card turns up in the wrong hand and the finesse loses. But when that happens, there was nothing for it anyway.

**Playing Towards the Tenace.** The key is playing from the right hand – towards the tenace. Never away from it. For the essence of the stratagem is to force the defender with the missing card to play *first*.

The next example is a case of 'same again':

$$A Q J \quad \boxed{\begin{array}{c} N \\ W \quad E \\ S \end{array}} \quad x\,x\,x\ (dummy)$$

This time, the tenace is in declarer's hand, and he plays from dummy, through South – hoping that he has the king.

If the queen holds, West crosses over to dummy with an entry in another suit, and repeats the finesse.

**When Defenders Lead.** In the next example there is no tenace, and therefore no finesse, but the same principle is at work.

$$A x \quad \boxed{\begin{array}{c} N \\ W \quad E \\ S \end{array}} \quad Q x\ (dummy)$$

Suppose that North leads a small card and it is dummy's turn to play. Which shall it be – the x or the queen?

Always the queen. Why? Because it may win and cannot lose. If South has the king, there is no way of winning more than one trick. But North may have it and then the queen will hold.

Alter the holding slightly.

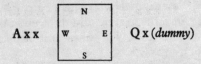

A x x     Q x (*dummy*)

If North leads, the position is as before. West goes up with
the queen and hopes for the best. This time, however, declarer
can attack the suit himself. He leads low towards dummy,
hoping that North has the king. If the hope is fulfilled, the
queen wins and the ace is still there for the next round.

What you have to bear in mind is that there is no alternative
– if you need two tricks from that combination.

The identical situation presents itself here:

x x     K x

If West needs a trick in the suit, he plays *up to* the king.
North may have the ace, and if so, the king will live to win a
trick. This is not a finesse, since there is no tenace, but the
mechanics are the same. Declarer hopes that a missing card is
where he wants it – *under* the card immediately below it. If his
hope is realized, he makes an extra trick. If he is unlucky, he
does not. But it is essentially a case of: heads I win, tails I do
not lose.

**The Double Finesse.** And now let us get back to our tenaces.
In French a tenace is called a *fourchette*, because of the gap – the
missing card – between the prongs of the fork. All the best
forks have more than one gap. So have some of the best
tenaces.

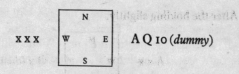

Assume that declarer needs all three tricks. Can it be done? If so, how? Try to visualize the distribution you need. Then find a way to take advantage of it.

Leaving out the possibility of a singleton honour with South, which is most unlikely, two cards have to be right. North must have both the king and the knave. Declarer plays up to the tenace, and puts on dummy's ten. If it holds, he returns to his hand and finesses once more.

Even when two tricks only are needed, the *double finesse* – the finesse against two honours – will prove its worth. The ten may fall to the king on the first round, making a second finesse unnecessary. And if the knave is with South the king may be with North. So long as both honours are not with South – in which case nothing can be done – two tricks are certain.

**Entries.** As with suit establishment, discussed in the last lesson, entries play a vital part in the technique of finessing. Everything hinges on leading from the right hand. And this sometimes requires a speck of forethought. A full deal will bring the point home.

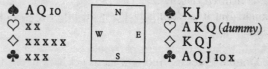

North leads a spade against six no-trumps by West. Imagine that you are declarer and plan your campaign. Ready?

What happened to that first trick? The slam may well depend on it.

Let us examine the situation. One trick will have to be lost to the ace of diamonds. Therefore, we cannot afford another loser, and that means that the king of clubs will have to be on the right side. If South has it, we can do nothing. If it is with North, all is well, for we can finesse.

The only snag is that we must be prepared to finesse *twice*. Five clubs are out against us and if the suit breaks evenly one of the defenders will have three. Why not North?

Against K x x, one finesse is not enough, for it will leave the holder with K x, and the king won't drop on the ace.

Play the hand out with a pack of cards. Deal North K x x and South x x in clubs and try not to lose a club trick.

As you see, the suit must be led twice from West's hand – *through* the king. That means that you need two entries. Where are they? Only the spades fill the bill, and if you win the first trick in dummy, you lose one of your two invaluable entries.

The answer is to overtake dummy's knave of spades with the queen. At the second trick finesse against the club king. Next, return to your own hand by overtaking the king of spades with the ace and repeat the club finesse. The king of clubs – always assuming that North was dealt K x x – will now drop on the ace.

Of course, life would be simpler if the closed hand (West) had the nine of clubs. After winning the first trick in his hand declarer would *run* the nine – playing low from dummy unless North produced the king.

Should the nine hold the trick, he would still be in his hand to repeat the finesse.

A still more obvious example would be:

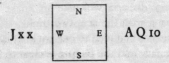

Jxx    W   N   E    A Q 10

West, declarer, leads the knave – not an x. If he holds the trick, he remains in his *own hand* to play through North's king once more.

Always bear in mind the *next* move.

**Covering Honours.** We now come to finesse situations which carry a message for the defence as well as for declarer.

When declarer leads a small card towards a tenace, the defence is powerless. The missing honour is right or wrong, and skill does not come into the picture. But sometimes declarer leads an honour.

The defender with a higher honour *covers*. He plays the queen on the knave, the knave on the ten and so on. Why? To force South to play a still higher card from dummy. That way, *two* enemy honours will be needed to kill *one* of his. Note what follows. With the higher cards out of the way, their juniors are *promoted*. And one or more of these may be held by the defence.

**Promotion.** To test the principle of promotion, try it out in an extreme case, one that is unlikely to arise in real life.

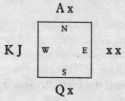

South leads the queen. West is in no doubt. He can see that unless he covers, declarer will take his knave with the queen, and then his king with the ace: two tricks. If he goes up with the king, declarer is confined to one trick. It is simple, because West has the knave and the picture is clear to him. But fundamentally, the same situation presents itself here:

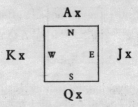

Again, if South leads the queen, West must cover, though it is not so apparent to him now that he can no longer see the knave.

The point is that West cannot *lose* by covering. If South has the knave, he certainly won't take his own queen with the ace. But if East has it, covering will promote his knave.

There is an ancient adage, which says: 'Cover an honour with an honour.' It does not apply in every situation, but it is sound tactics most of the time.

Here is another example:

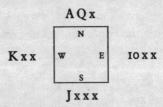

South leads the knave. If West plays low, he runs it, finesses again, and makes all the tricks. If West covers, East's ten is master after two rounds.

Naturally, if South leads a small card, West plays low, too. Going up with the king can promote nothing, for declarer cannot win a trick with his x and must play high from dummy anyway.

The next example is a little more complicated. But it is based on the same principle – promotion.

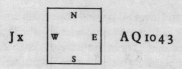

West plays the knave, hoping to find North with the king. If the suit breaks 3–3, he will make all five tricks. And what if the king is right, but the distribution is 4–2? Say that North has K x?

That is where the spotlight turns on North. He can wrest a trick from declarer – or he can let it slip through his fingers.

The correct defence is to cover the knave with the king. Why? It makes no difference to North's hand – for his king is lost anyway – but all the difference to his partner. If North has K x, the distribution will be

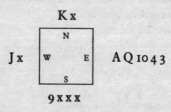

Now go through the motions. If North plays low, West runs the knave and picks up the king on the next round. South's nine will eventually fall to the ten.

If North covers, South will live to make his nine.

Take it step by step. The first trick will absorb three honours – the ace, the king and the knave. The second trick will be won by the queen and the third one – not the fourth, mark you – by the ten.

By going up with the king on the knave, North promotes South's nine. This happens because declarer parts with *two* honours – the ace and knave – to capture one, the king.

**When not to Cover.** Covering honours is not a convention or a tradition. It is based on simple logic – the logic of drawing two honours for one. There are exceptions to the general rule – logical exceptions, which, given a little time, every player can work out for himself.

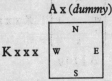

South leads the queen, but West does not cover, because he is *longer* in the suit than dummy. The king cannot be caught. The ace will have to be played on the second round while the king will remain intact – a master card, controlling the third round. The position may be:

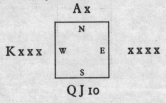

As you can see, South is kept to two tricks if West holds off, but makes all three if the queen is covered by the king.

Here is a similar situation with East as the focus of attention

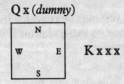

If the queen is led from dummy, East plays low. The finesse against the king can only be taken twice, and that is not enough to capture him. The deal may be:

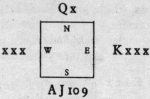

Q x

x x x    W    E    K x x x

A J 10 9

**When Declarer Leads from a Sequence.** Another occasion for not covering is when declarer leads from a sequence.

Q J 10 9 (*dummy*)

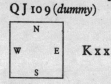

W    E    K x x

East plays low to dummy's queen, because there is *nothing to promote*. Every card that could be promoted is on view – in dummy.

As long as you remember that the one and only purpose in covering is promotion of a lesser card – in your own hand or in partner's – you will find the right answer in most situations. A few, here and there, will still elude you – until you gain more experience.

Meanwhile, you may be consoled by the thought that bridge would lose one of its many charms if it presented fewer opportunities for mistakes.

## Exercises

1. ♠ A K
   ♡ A Q J 9 x
   ◇ 10 x x
   ♣ K Q J

   ♠ J x x x
   ♡ 10 x x
   ◇ Q x x
   ♣ A 10 x

The contract is three no-trumps by South. West leads a diamond from A J x x, finds his partner with the king, and collects the first four tricks. He then switches to a spade.

(a) What N S cards should make up the sixth trick?

(b) What N S cards should make up the seventh trick, assuming that defenders play low?

2. ♠ K Q J x
   ♡ A Q 10
   ◇ K Q
   ♣ A K Q J

   ♠ A x x
   ♡ x x x x
   ◇ A x
   ♣ x x x x

The contract is six no-trumps by South. West opens a diamond.

(a) What N S cards should make up the first trick?

(b) What N S cards should make up the second trick?

3. J x x (*dummy*)

Declarer leads knave from dummy.

K x x

Should East cover?

4. ♠ A x x x
   ♡ K x
   ◊ K x x
   ♣ K x x x

The contract is three no-trumps by South.

West leads a small heart.

What card should South play from dummy?

   ♠ K x
   ♡ x x x
   ◊ A x x
   ♣ A Q J x x

5. ♠ A K x x
   ♡ Q x
   ◊ K x x
   ♣ K x x x

The contract is again three no-trumps by South, and West leads a small heart.
What card should South play from dummy?

   ♠ x x
   ♡ J x x
   ◊ A x x
   ♣ A Q J x x

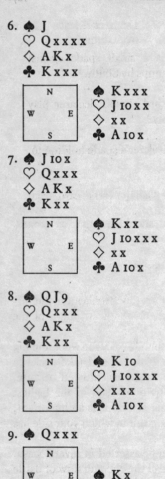

6. ♠ J
  ♡ Q x x x x
  ◇ A K x
  ♣ K x x

  N ♠ K x x x
  ♡ J 10 x x
  ◇ x x
  ♣ A 10 x

The contract is three no-trumps by South, and West opens a diamond. South wins with the king on the table and leads the knave of spades.

Should East cover?

7. ♠ J 10 x
  ♡ Q x x x
  ◇ A K x
  ♣ K x x

  N ♠ K x x
  ♡ J 10 x x x
  ◇ x x
  ♣ A 10 x

As in the previous example, West opens a diamond against three no-trumps, South wins in dummy and leads the knave of spades.

Should East cover?

8. ♠ Q J 9
  ♡ Q x x x
  ◇ A K x
  ♣ K x x

  N ♠ K 10
  ♡ J 10 x x x
  ◇ x x x
  ♣ A 10 x

The contract and the opening lead are as in 7 above. Declarer leads the queen of spades from dummy.

Should East cover?

9. ♠ Q x x x

  N ♠ K x

South opens the bidding with four spades and all pass. West's opening lead is won in dummy. Declarer plays the queen of spades.

Should East cover?

10.♠ J x
♡ Q 10 x x
◇ K Q x
♣ J x x x

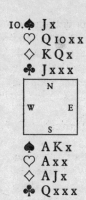

West opens a small spade against three no-trumps by South.

(*a*) What card should declarer play from dummy?

♠ A K x
♡ A x x
◇ A J x
♣ Q x x x

(*b*) Alter declarer's spade holding to: A 10 x.

Should he play the same card from dummy as in (*a*)?

## LESSON X

# CARD PLAY

**Suit Contracts.** A suit contract sometimes makes for the discomfiture of aces. Often it brings about the triumph of the deuce.

At all times the x's play an important role, for when the big cards have fallen, the small ones grow big and take tricks in their own right. In suit contracts this is accentuated because, from the first, the lowest trump is the master of the highest cards in the other three suits. That is why it is so important, during the auction, to select a trump suit in which your side has numerical superiority.

In the play, that superiority can be asserted in several ways, but all hinge on the power to control the ebb and flow of battle which declarer enjoys through his privileged suit.

**Control.** Examine these N S hands:

♠ x x x
♡ x x
◇ A x x
♣ K Q x x x

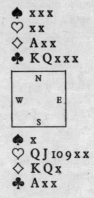

♠ x
♡ Q J 10 9 x x
◇ K Q x
♣ A x x

It is easy to make ten tricks in hearts and yet it is impossible to make nine tricks in no-trumps. There is no guard in spades and that is fatal – in no-trumps. But with hearts as trumps, South takes control of the situation at the second trick. By ruffing the second spade he wrests the initiative from the defence. That ruff does not yield an extra trick. Declarer expects to make four of his six trumps anyway. But gaining the lead gives him command of the play.

**Drawing Trumps.** Assuming a spade opening and continuation, South wins the second trick and plays – trumps. Why? It is important to understand the reason for drawing trumps.

Just as declarer's small trumps enable him to ruff defenders' high cards in the other suits, so defenders' trumps enable them to do the same to declarer. That is why they must be removed.

Look at the hand again. East and West between them have the ace, the king and three small hearts. And it is the small ones that matter. South must lose tricks to the ace and king in any case. But the x's are E W *losers* and must be extracted. Otherwise declarer's winners in the side-suits may be ruffed.

Before South can get at the defenders' small trumps, he will
have to drive out the ace and king. So he must lead trumps
three times in all, assuming the likely 3–2 break.

Finally, after drawing the enemy's last trump, and not
before, South will cash his winners in clubs and diamonds.

The next example is on the same lines.

♠ x x x x
♡ x x
◇ K x
♣ K J 10 x x

♠ A K x x
♡ A x
◇ A x x
♣ Q x x x

The obvious contract is four spades, but it may be instruc-
tive first of all to consider three no-trumps.

Declarer can make game on one condition: that he drives out
the ace of clubs *before* he has to part with the ace of hearts. If
West opens a heart, as well he may, South is helpless. It
becomes a race between hearts and clubs, and the advantage
must lie with the defence, which has the first move – the
opening lead.

Turn to four spades. South wins the first heart, lays down
the ace and king of spades, and attacks the clubs. He can lose
one heart only, for on the third round he ruffs. As in the last
example, trumps enable him to take control.

But observe that, this time, declarer does not draw *all* the E W
trumps. He takes two rounds only, leaving one trump out in
enemy hands. The reason is that defenders have one winning

trump anyway. It makes no difference to South whether East –
or West – uses his winning trump to ruff a club or to take a
small trump. As we saw above, it is defenders' *losing* trumps
that must be drawn – not the winners.

We have assumed that the outstanding trumps were divided
3–2, something like Q 10 x with West and J x with East.

This is a good place to emphasize the importance of having a
lot of trumps – eight or nine at least – between the two hands.
Take one of dummy's spades away, and the play becomes
much more difficult. Declarer cannot settle down to the clubs
while two trumps are still out against him. And he dare not
play three rounds of trumps, in case they break badly.

What if he takes a chance and runs up against a 4–2 spade
break? Give one of dummy's trumps to West and go through
the play. South cashes the ace and king, then loses a trump
trick to West. East shows out, of course. But it is too late for
declarer to do anything about it. West is on play and he, too,
has counted the spades. He and South have one each, and his is
the master. West draws the last trump and reels off his hearts.
He can do that now, for he has taken control.

That is the danger of a suit contract when the N S hands
have not enough trumps. Control may pass to a defender who
has as many trumps as declarer. The roles are then reversed. It
is one of the defenders, not declarer, who draws trumps and
dictates the play.

Hence the importance of the quantitative – as against the
qualitative – aspect of the trump suit.

**Ruffing in Dummy.** The control factor – the ability to seize the
initiative by ruffing an ace with a deuce – is only one of the
advantages of a suit contract. Another is the opportunity it
offers to make tricks by ruffing in dummy.

Here is a typical example:

&spades; x
&hearts; x x x x
&diams; A x x x
&clubs; A x x x

&spades; A x x
&hearts; A K x x
&diams; K x x
&clubs; K x x

In no-trumps declarer is most unlikely to collect nine tricks. Regardless of the opening lead, the stuffing just is not there.

But in four hearts ten tricks can be gathered without any special luck. Declarer ruffs two spades in dummy, after cashing the ace, and still makes three trump tricks in his own hand – asssuming the probable 3–2 break in trumps. Four top tricks in the minors bring the total up to ten.

**Making the Trumps Separately.** To simplify the issue, look at this combination:

x x x x

A K Q J

In no-trumps it will yield four tricks and four only. Make the suit trumps and it may produce six or seven. In addition to the four top tricks in the closed hand, declarer may be able to ruff two or three losers in dummy – if dummy is short in something.

It is the fact that the trumps in the closed hand, and in dummy, can be made *separately*, that allows declarer to make additional tricks in a suit contract.

Of course, the more trumps there are in dummy, the better. And, of course, it helps a lot to have shortages – a void, a singleton or doubletons – on the table. Hence the 1–2–3 scale in Lesson IV.

The tendency to steer hands of the 4–3–3–3 type into no-trump contracts is due to their lack of ruffing value. Conversely, distributional hands, with a fit for partner, play best in a suit.

**Preparing Ruffs.** With a void in dummy – or a singleton opposite an ace in the closed hand – ruffs come almost automatically. More often, declarer must undertake a little preparation.

♠ x x
♡ K x x
♢ x x x x
♣ A x x x

N
W    E
S

♠ A x x x
♡ A Q J 10 x
♢ A J
♣ J x

West leads a club against four hearts. Looking round – before playing his first card – South sees eight tricks. To make his contract he needs two ruffs in dummy. That will enable him to win *seven* trump tricks – five in his own hand and two more on the table.

Since he cannot ruff anything at the second trick, declarer plays spades to create a shortage in dummy.

If the defence persists with clubs, he trumps the third one in his hand, ruffs a spade on the table, and enters his hand again with the ace of diamonds to lead his last spade.

If West follows, South must ruff, with *the king*. For no more spades are out and if South ruffs low, East will over-ruff.

**Defence Against Ruffing.** The hand presents little difficulty – against a club opening. But suppose that West leads a diamond?

This is where defenders have a chance to shine. Put yourself in West's place and conjure up a scheme to break the contract. It is true that you have not seen your hand, but that does not matter. It is the principle that counts.

As before, South leads spades and you, sitting West, come in at the second trick. What do you play?

A trump. South wins and ruffs a spade. But before he can get back to his own hand, he must let your side in again, for he has no entry, outside hearts. And as soon as you get in, you lead another trump.

It amounts to this: declarer has three trumps in dummy and he wants to ruff two spades. If your side leads trumps twice in good time, *one* trump only will be left for *one* ruff.

When declarer schemes to make his trumps separately, defenders lead trumps themselves to knock them together – to reduce dummy's ruffing value.

How do E W know South's plan of campaign? Firstly, because he does not draw trumps himself. That is already

somewhat suspicious, because it is usually in his interest to
remove the hostile trumps. Secondly, and this is even more
important, declarer's attack on dummy's shortage – as in the
last example – reveals his intentions.

Every case must be treated on its merits, but it is often right
for the defenders to play trumps in a suit contract, when there
are shortages on the table.

**'Ruffing Out' a Long Suit.** Declarer usually has more trumps
than his dummy. That is why he tries to ruff on the table, not
in his hand. His own trumps will take tricks anyway. Dummy's
will not – without a little scheming.

♠ J x
♡ A x x
◇ A x
♣ A K x x x x

♠ A K Q 10 x x
♡ x x x
◇ Q x x
♣ x

West opens a heart against six spades. South can see ten top
tricks and needs two more. Dummy's good-looking clubs provide the answer. By ruffing, declarer can establish two long
clubs. E W have six clubs between them, and even if they
break 4–2, South can 'ruff them out'. Let us go through it
together.

Declarer rises with dummy's ace of hearts, leads a top club
and ruffs a small club in his hand. Crossing to dummy with the
knave of spades, he ruffs another club – high – in case West

started with a doubleton and is in a position to over-ruff. All that now remains is to draw trumps. The rest is a formality. South enters dummy with the ace of diamonds and drops the last enemy club – if either defender had four originally – on the king.

Whenever dummy has entries and a long suit, it is always worth examining the possibility of setting it up. Declarer can work it out by asking himself these questions: how many times shall I have to ruff, assuming a reasonable distribution? Have I enough entries in dummy to get at the suit often enough, and to cross over again after I have established it?

**Entries and Timing.** The entries, of course, must not be handled thoughtlessly. In our last example, South needs two entries apart from the ace of clubs. He has them in the knave of trumps and the ace of diamonds. But he must not use the diamond ace *first*. Can you see why?

South must draw trumps *before* he can cash the two long clubs. Otherwise someone will ruff. If dummy had three trumps, declarer could draw trumps, *ending* on the table. With two only, it can't be done, for East or West must have more trumps than dummy.

**The Same, Only Different.** Now have a shot at this one:

♠ Q x x
♡ x x x
◇ x x
♣ A K J x x

|   | N |   |
|---|---|---|
| W |   | E |
|   | S |   |

♠ A K J 10 x
♡ J 10 x
◇ A J 10 x
♣ x

Four spades is the contract. The defence takes the first three hearts and shifts to a diamond.

How do you go about making the rest of the tricks? There are eight winners on top. Any ideas about the other two?

Here is a tip. Combine the technique of the last example with what you learned in the lesson on Finessing.

Try to set up the clubs. Assume the likely 4–3 break and hope that the queen is where you want her – under the tenace. Finesse against the queen. If the knave holds – as half the time it will – ruff a small club. Now draw trumps, *ending* with the queen on the table. You can do it this time, because there is no reason for either defender to have more than three trumps.

Obviously, the queen must not be played to the first or second trump trick. She must be left to the end as the vital entry to the clubs.

In no-trumps the fifth club could still be established – but only after conceding a trick, for East or West must have four clubs. In a suit contract that loser can be ruffed. It does not make an extra winner. But it avoids a loser.

**Forcing Declarer.** It is time to espouse, once more, the cause of the defenders. We have examined already one weapon in their armoury – leading trumps, when declarer tries to ruff losers in dummy. Another is the force – the attack on the trumps in the closed hand. The idea is to make declarer *too* short in trumps. And the best time to do it, usually, is when one of the defenders is fairly long in trumps himself.

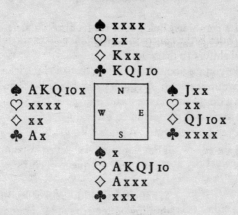

```
                ♠ x x x x
                ♡ x x
                ◇ K x x
                ♣ K Q J 10
♠ A K Q 10 x      N        ♠ J x x
♡ x x x x               ♡ x x
◇ x x       W     E     ◇ Q J 10 x
♣ A x               S    ♣ x x x x
                ♠ x
                ♡ A K Q J 10
                ◇ A x x x
                ♣ x x x
```

On the face of it, South should have no difficulty in making four hearts. He has five certain trump tricks, two diamond tricks and three club tricks.

West opens and continues spades. South ruffs, and immediately his impressive trump holding shrinks – quantitively – to West's level. Four each.

Declarer cannot afford to draw all the trumps, for if he does, West will have three spades, to cash when he comes in with the ace of clubs.

If South drives out the club ace first, before playing trumps, West will force him again with another spade. After that West will have *more* trumps than South.

You can work out the consequences. In a race between West and South, the advantage will lie with West – for he is one move ahead.

The forcing game often suggests itself when dummy is short in trumps. It rarely succeeds when dummy has four trumps or more. Then declarer does not mind being forced, even if he started with four trumps only. That is why it is so important, in bidding, to find a fit – a suit which partner likes. And that is why responder should never support the opener on a doubleton.

Against a combined holding of six trumps, an alert defence can play a forcing game with devastating effect.

## Exercises

1. ♠ Q x
   ♡ x x
   ◇ A J x x x
   ♣ K x x x

The contract is seven diamonds. West opens the queen of clubs.

What card should declarer lead from dummy after drawing opponents' trumps?

   ♠ A K x
   ♡ A x x
   ◇ K Q x x x
   ♣ A x

2. ♠ 9 x x x
   ♡ A x x x
   ◇ x x
   ♣ A x x

The contract is three spades. West leads a heart.

(a) In which hand should South win the trick?

(b) What suit should he lead next?

   ♠ K Q J 10
   ♡ K x x
   ◇ K Q x x
   ♣ x x

3.  ♠ K x x x x x
    ♡ A x
    ◇ A x x                    The contract is six hearts. West
    ♣ A x                      opens a trump.

                               (a) In which hand should South win
                               the trick?

    ♠ A                        (b) What suit should he lead next?
    ♡ K Q J 10 x x
    ◇ Q x x
    ♣ Q x x

4.  ♠ x x
    ♡ x x
    ◇ K x x                    The contract is three diamonds. West
    ♣ A Q x x x x              leads a trump.

                               (a) In which hand should South win
                               the trick?

    ♠ x x x                    (b) What card should he play next
    ♡ A x x                    from his hand, and from dummy?
    ◇ A Q J x x
    ♣ x x

5.
&spades; K x x
&hearts; x x
&diams; K Q x
&clubs; A Q 10 9 x

&spades; Q J 10 x x
&hearts; A x x x
&diams; x
&clubs; K J x

The bidding was:

| N | E | S | W |
|---|---|---|---|
| one | no | four | no |
| club | bid | hearts | bid |

West leads the queen of spades, which holds. The knave of spades is ruffed by South, who leads the king of hearts. West goes up with the ace and East shows out. What suit should West lead?

6. &spades; J x x
&hearts; Q x
&diams; A x x
&clubs; Q J 10 x x

&spades; A K Q x
&hearts; x
&diams; J x x x
&clubs; A K x x

The contract is four spades. West leads the king of hearts, and then the ace. What card should South play from his hand to the second trick?

7. ♠ K x x
   ♡ K x
   ♢ x x x
   ♣ x x x x x

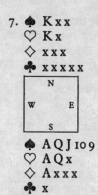

West leads a trump against four spades by South. Declarer has nine tricks. How should he plan to make his tenth trick?

♠ A Q J 10 9
♡ A Q x
♢ A x x x
♣ x

8. ♠ x
   ♡ K J 10 8
   ♢ A x x x
   ♣ x x x x

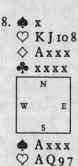

West leads the queen of clubs against four hearts by South. East plays the king and South the ace. How should declarer play the hand?

♠ A x x x
♡ A Q 9 7
♢ x
♣ A x x x

9. ♠ x x x
   ♡ x x x
   ◇ x
   ♣ A Q 10 x x x

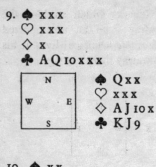

   ♠ Q x x
   ♡ x x x
   ◇ A J 10 x
   ♣ K J 9

West opens the queen of hearts against two spades by South. Declarer wins in his hand and leads a small diamond which East takes with the ten.

What should East do now?

10. ♠ x x
    ♡ x x x x
    ◇ x x x
    ♣ A Q 10 x

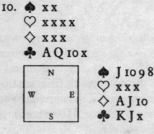

    ♠ J 10 9 8
    ♡ x x x
    ◇ A J 10
    ♣ K J x

The contract and the opening lead are as in 9. Declarer wins in his hand and leads a club, playing the ten from dummy.

What should East play when he comes in with the club knave?

## LESSON XI

# CARD PLAY

**Opening Leads.** In this lesson the spotlight is on defence. This begins with the opening lead and the decision must be made before dummy comes into view.

Many leads are standardized. Others must be suited to the occasion.

**Sequences.** In the first category come hands containing a sequence of three or more honours. West just leads the top – the king from K Q J, the queen from Q J 10, the knave from J 10 9. That is a safe lead because it is unlikely to lose a trick.

Cast your mind back to the tenaces which studded the lesson on finesse. By leading away from an unsupported honour, a defender may be playing *into* a tenace. Even if his cards are well placed, he may throw away the advantage.

Left to play the suit himself, South can only make two tricks in figure 1, and one trick in 2. By leading away from his queen or king, West presents declarer with an extra trick both times.

Other things being equal, avoid playing away from unsupported (not in sequence) honours. In no-trump contracts, and also when partner has made a bid, other things are not always equal.

**Lead from Length Against No-trumps.** Let us start with no-trumps. The defence rests on the theory that no-trump contracts are rarely broken by brute force – aces and kings. The best line of attack is to lead from *length* and to establish one or more small cards – before declarer can develop his quota of tricks.

Here is a typical three no-trump contract.

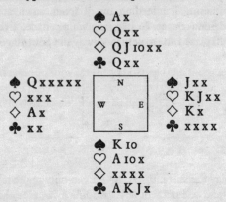

West opens a small spade and drives out one of declarer's two stoppers.

South cannot come to nine tricks without bringing in the diamonds and attacks the suit immediately. East wins with the king and returns a spade. This kills declarer's remaining stopper, and when West gains the lead with his ace of diamonds he can cash four winning spades.

Note these points:

West leads from an unsupported honour, because spades are his long suit and he hopes to set up his small cards before South can gather nine tricks.

East returns a spade, because the two defenders should always try to combine – to keep up the pressure on the same weak spot. There are exceptions, but it is generally best to play back partner's suit.

It is a typical no-trump 'race' in which both sides strive to set up their respective suits. Each side has two stoppers – the ace and king – in the other's suit. The defence wins owing to the advantage of the opening lead which puts it one move ahead of declarer.

The accepted lead from length is the fourth highest. There is a reason for making it just that, but it touches on matters too advanced for this course. In selecting your x, make it the fourth highest (Q 8 6 4 2) and don't worry just yet about the whys and wherefores.

If your long suit has been bid by one of your opponents during the auction, it is usually best to try something else. Partner is not likely to have much in that quarter, and the lead will only help declarer.

**Leading Partner's Suit.** A different situation arises when a suit has been bid by partner. Generally speaking, lead it. Again, there are exceptions. With a holding headed by the A K in another suit, you can play the king 'to look round'. More often than not, the temptation won't be there and your problem will be to select for your opening the right card of partner's suit.

This, too, is largely standardized.

From a sequence or from two touching honours, play the top.

From four or more – J x x x or x x x x x – the fourth highest.

From three small ones or from a doubleton, the highest – except from K x x, Q x x or J x x. Then the small one.

This gives partner a general picture. Seeing the eight or nine, he knows that you have neither four, nor an honour.

The deuce or the three-spot suggests an honour – or else length in the suit. A look at his own hand and at dummy will often help partner to fill in the background.

Against no-trumps it is correct to lead the lowest from A x x. But in a suit contract, play the ace of partner's suit; then the next highest card.

Declarer may have the king and dummy a singleton. Or the king may be bare in either hand. To underlead the ace would then cost a certain trick; you may not be able to make your ace later, because it will be ruffed.

In no-trumps such situations are unlikely to arise. Declarer is pretty certain to have a guard in a suit bid by opponents, for he expects it to be led; and you will always be able to make your ace.

In a suit contract, however, there is nothing unusual about a singleton.

**Suit Establishment in Defence.** Here is another situation in which no-trumps and suit contracts call for different tactics by the defence. This time, partner passes throughout and you hold:

♠ x x x    ♡ x x    ♢ x x x    ♣ A K x x x

Against a suit contract the obvious lead is the king of clubs. Note, by the way, that it is the king, not the ace. That is an exception to the general rule, which is to lead the highest of touching honours. From A K, the king is more informative. It holds the trick and this usually tells partner that the ace (it may be the queen) is behind the king – even if, for some reason, you switch to another suit.

Against no-trumps, the correct lead is a *small* club. The reason is that your main preoccupation is to set up the x's, and for this you will need partner's help. Unless he has at least one entry, there is little hope of defeating the contract. But it may be that declarer will have to give up the lead to partner before he can develop nine tricks. And it is vital that when this happens, he should have a club to play. It is also vital that you should have an entry.

Sitting West, the player on lead, you expect declarer or dummy – both maybe – to hold three clubs. You must lose one trick anyway – unless, of course, East happens to hold the queen. So, opening a small one does not cost a trick. But it allows East to return the suit, even if he started with a doubleton. And it preserves an entry for you *at the right time* – when your ace and king can draw the outstanding clubs, thereby setting up the x's.

Look at all four hands and try to break the contract.

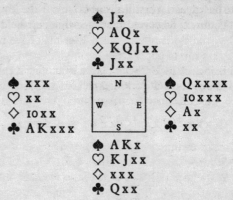

First lead a small club. Next time, try the king. As you will see, the contract is impossible against the correct lead – and unbreakable against any other. Go through the motions carefully to study, in practice, the technique of suit-establishment in defence.

**Leads from Suits Headed by Tenaces.** From combinations headed by the A K J, lead the king. This applies both to suit contracts and to no-trumps. Even if East has a doubleton, he can still return the suit. West hopes for a distribution like:

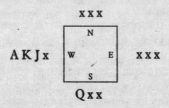

He opens the king and switches to some other suit. When East gains the lead, he plays through South's queen and the defence collects all four tricks.

From A Q J x x, the correct opening lead in no-trump contracts is the queen. The idea is to drive out the king at the first trick. If the ace is played first, declarer may hold up the king till, say, the third round. Then East may have no more cards left in that suit to put West in.

Observe that declarer dare not hold up the king if the queen is opened. If he does, West switches, and the king becomes finessible.

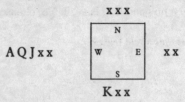

When East gains the lead, he plays *through* the king into his partner's tenace.

In a suit contract leads from an A Q combination should be avoided altogether. But if the suit must be led, the correct opening is the ace.

**Singletons and Passive Leads.** A singleton is often a good lead against suit contracts, because it paves the way for a ruff – or even several ruffs. Partner may have the ace of the suit led. Or he may come in with something else before declarer can draw trumps.

There are times when no good lead suggests itself. In such cases a trump may be the way out. The very fact that declarer is in a suit contract indicates that he hopes to make tricks by ruffing in dummy. An early attack on the trumps will reduce his opportunities.

Now, let us take a hand like

♠ K x   ♡ K x x x   ◇ A J x x   ♣ 9 x x

Against a spade contract no lead looks attractive. A club is best, because even if it does no good, it is unlikely to cost anything. The card to play is the nine, 'top of nothing'.

Now suppose that the contract is three no-trumps and that South called hearts and diamonds on the way round.

On that bidding, a lead from either red suit is likely to help declarer. So, once more, West takes a purely passive line and falls back on his top club.

The moral is: when no good lead is available, choose the one least likely to lose a trick.

Finally, let us consider a real teaser.

West holds:

*Bidding*

| | S | W | N | E |
|---|---|---|---|---|
| ♠ 9 x | S | W | N | E |
| ♡ K J x x x | One heart | No bid | One spade | No bid |
| ◇ A Q x | One no-trump | — | — | — |
| ♣ K J x | | | | |

No prospect pleases, but which is the least forbidding?

A heart would be the natural lead, but declarer has bid hearts and probably has something like A Q 10 x. Sitting over him, West can only lose by leading into a tenace.

Both clubs and diamonds are uninviting. West does not know who has the missing honours and would like to wait for the suits to be opened up by declarer.

In hearts, West fears to lead into a tenace. In clubs and diamonds he is reluctant to lead away from one.

That leaves spades, the suit called by North. And it is not a bad opening – because the lead will be *through* the strength. There is quite a chance that East will have something in that suit, since declarer did not support it in the auction. What is more, East's cards are likely to be in the right place, *over* dummy's spades.

Just as a defender should always avoid leading *into* strength, so he should welcome the opportunity to lead *through* it. If partner has nothing useful in the suit, little harm will be done. But if he turns up with the right cards, an imaginative opening may prove deadly.

The more you play bridge, the more scope you will find for 'inspired' plays – and the more you will enjoy the game.

## Exercises

The bidding was:

|  | S (dealer) | N |
| --- | --- | --- |
|  | One spade | Two diamonds |
|  | Two no-trumps | Three no-trumps |

Sitting West, what do you lead from:

| 1. | 2. | 3. | 4. |
| --- | --- | --- | --- |
| ♠ x x x | ♠ 10 x | ♠ K J 9 x | ♠ J x |
| ♡ A K x | ♡ A x x | ♡ K J x | ♡ A Q J 10 x |
| ◇ x x x | ◇ K Q J 10 | ◇ Q x x | ◇ x x x |
| ♣ J 10 9 x | ♣ x x x x | ♣ x x x | ♣ J 10 9 |

The bidding was:

| N | E | S | W |
| --- | --- | --- | --- |
| One club | One diamond | One spade | No bid |
| Two spades | No bid | Four spades | No bid |
| No bid | No bid |  |  |

Sitting West what do you lead from:

| 5. | 6. | 7. |
| --- | --- | --- |
| ♠ x x x | ♠ x x x | ♠ x x x |
| ♡ x | ♡ x x x | ♡ x x x |
| ◇ J x x x | ◇ A x x | ◇ K x x |
| ♣ Q x x x x | ♣ Q J x x | ♣ Q J x x |

8.  ♠ J 10 9          The contract is six no-trumps by
    ♡ x x x          South. Sitting West what do you
    ◇ A Q x x x      lead?
    ♣ J x

The bidding was:

| N | E | S | W |
|---|---|---|---|
| — | — | | |
| | | One spade | No bid |
| Four spades | No bid | Six spades | — |

Sitting West, what do you lead from:

> 9.  ♠ x x x
>     ♡ x
>     ◇ J x x x x
>     ♣ J x x

The bidding was:

|  S  |  N  |
|-----|-----|
| One no-trump | Three no-trumps |

Sitting West, what do you lead from:

10.  ♠ Q J 10 9          11.  ♠ K Q 10 9 2
     ♡ 10 9                   ♡ 7 6
     ◇ K J 4 3 2             ◇ A K 2
     ♣ 7 5                    ♣ 4 3 2

12.  ♠ A 2               13.  ♠ A Q 4 2
     ♡ Q 10 8 6 4 2           ♡ 7 6
     ◇ J 10 9                 ◇ J 10 9 5
     ♣ 7 6                    ♣ 10 8 2

The bidding was:

|  S  |  N  |
| --- | --- |
| One heart | Four hearts |

Sitting West, what do you lead from:

| 14. | ♠ x | 15. | ♠ K x x |
| --- | --- | --- | --- |
|  | ♡ Q J 9 2 |  | ♡ x x x |
|  | ◇ Q J 10 9 |  | ◇ Q x x x |
|  | ♣ A x x x |  | ♣ K J x |

## LESSON XII

# CARD PLAY

**Tactics in Defence.** Our attention is still focused on the defence, but West has had his share of the limelight and the time has come to consider East, the third man.

East has an advantage over his partner. When he comes to play to the first trick, he can see twenty-seven cards – his own, dummy's and West's lead. He is less likely to make a bloomer than West, who opens in the dark.

Cooperation is the first and most important rule in defence. East and West must pull together. If West decides to develop a suit, East throws his weight in support.

In playing to the first trick, East pursues a twofold objective: he tries to show West the nature of his holding; and he endeavours to promote West's line of attack. If the lead looks like a singleton, East seeks a chance to give his partner a ruff. If, in no-trumps, West opens from length, East does his best to drive out declarer's high cards, so as to set up partner's suit.

**Third Hand Plays High.** West opens a spade against three no-trumps.

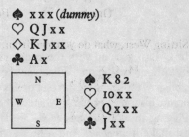

♠ x x x (*dummy*)
♡ Q J x x
♢ K J x x
♣ A x

       ♠ K 8 2
       ♡ 10 x x
       ♢ Q x x x
       ♣ J x x

East plays the king – his highest. If it holds, he returns the eight – his next highest.

There is an ancient adage at bridge: Third hand plays high.

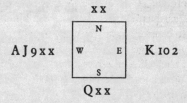

       x x

A J 9 x x         K 10 2

       Q x x

West opens a small spade. If East plays high and returns the ten, defenders make all five tricks. Should he falter, failing to go up with the king, declarer will make his unmakeable queen.

Now observe what happens if East wins with the king, but then returns the deuce.

West will take the trick with nine, but he will 'miss' the ten. He will assume that declarer started with Q 10 x x, and may abandon the suit altogether – instead of collecting three more tricks.

Like everything else in bridge, the third-hand-plays-high rule is applied logically – not blindly. Compare these two situations:

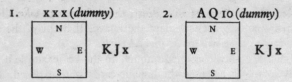

1.      x x x *(dummy)*      2.      A Q 10 *(dummy)*

     W   E    K J x        W   E    K J x

In 1, East goes up with the king on his partner's lead of the suit without hesitation. Whatever the contract, East tries to establish West's holding – to set up his small cards or maybe to promote his queen or ten or whatever he led from.

Playing the king *cannot lose* – for if South has the ace, he must make it anyway. And if he has the A Q, he is bound to make both.

In 2, East will go up with the king *only* if declarer puts on the queen from dummy. Should he play the ten, East will win with the knave. What is more, he will switch to some other suit. To return it, would present declarer with a trick which he could not possibly win himself.

The above diagram presents a clearcut situation. Perhaps the next one is not so obvious.

♠ Q 10 x *(dummy)*

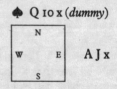

     W   E    A J x

West opens a small one and South plays the ten from dummy. What should East do?

The automatic reaction may be to go up with the ace because of the 'Third hand high' rule. A moment's thought will show that this play can only lose.

If South has the king, he must win one trick in the suit anyway. But he will take *two* if East goes up with the ace – his own king *and* dummy's queen.

Should the king be with West, the defence can take all the tricks – so long as East plays the knave. If he plays the ace, dummy's queen will live to make a trick.

That is a finesse against dummy. In the last example it was easy to spot it since all the honour cards were exposed. This time, the king is missing. But the idea is the same. East hopes that his partner has the king – but he has nothing to lose if South has it.

In short, it is generally correct for the third man to play his highest. But when there is an honour in the suit on the table, East finesses against it.

When in doubt, apply common sense and you won't be far out.

**Every Card Tells a Story.** The order in which the cards are played has a meaning for the defenders.

We have noted already that one of the best leads is the top of a sequence. The top, you will observe – not the second or third highest. This way, seeing West's queen, East will know that the knave is behind it. Seeing the knave, he will deduce the ten. Every card tells a story.

In playing to his partner's leads East also conveys information – but the other way round. With touching cards he selects the *lowest*. It works like this:

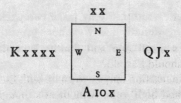

On West's lead, East goes up with his highest – naturally. But the queen and knave are *equally* high. And yet it makes all the difference which card is played.

**Inference.** If South takes the knave with the ace, West will *know* that his partner has the queen. Obviously; for if South had it, he would not have wasted an ace where a queen would have served just as well.

But should East play the queen, there will be no *inference* for West. South would still have to win with the ace if he had A J.

Of course, when East comes to lead his own suit, he opens the top of a sequence – or the higher of two touching cards. But in following to partner's suit the contrary is right. And both times, the idea is the same – to give partner as much information as possible. This courtesy should not be extended to declarer.

**Second Hand Plays Low.** The adage: 'Third hand plays high' is balanced by another: 'Second hand plays low.' And there is more to it than withholding information. Test it:

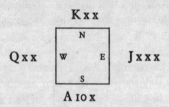

K x x

Q x x    J x x x

A 10 x

Left to himself, South can only make two tricks. But if he leads an x towards dummy and West hops up with the queen, South can finesse against East's knave next time and take three tricks.

South clearly intends to play dummy's king in any case. So why should West throw his queen on it?

Maybe that is obvious. But perhaps it is easier to go wrong here:

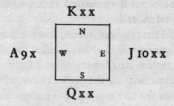

K x x

A 9 x    W    E    J 10 x x

Q x x

If South plays small, West must not go up with the ace. Should he do so, declarer will win an extra trick. Consider: whatever West does, the king is bound to make. But the queen is not. So long as West does not part with it prematurely, that ace will always remain in position to kill the queen.

Unless there is some compelling reason for seizing the initiative at a given moment, a defender should avoid wasting his aces on x's. Aces are made to take kings and queens – not deuces.

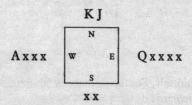

K J

A x x x    W    E    Q x x x x

x x

South leads one of his x's and West again plays low – to give declarer a guess. If he plays the ace, each side will take one trick. If he follows small, South, not knowing where the queen is, *may* put on the knave, losing both tricks.

As we learned in the lesson on finessing, a defender is usually right to cover an honour. He does so to promote a lesser card in his own or in partner's hand. But when declarer leads a deuce – or a five – West can't do much in the way of promotion.

**Signalling.** As soon as dummy goes down, declarer can see all
the cards on his side. Aware of all the strength and all the
weaknesses, he is well placed to take charge of combined
operations. A defender can only see half the cards on his side –
yet it is essential that he should coordinate his movements with
partner's. To bring about this coordination the defence has
evolved a partnership language.

Inference is the basis. Some of the language we have learned
to interpret already – as when we read partner's opening leads.

By extending the technique, we can tell partner whether we
like his leads or whether we should welcome a switch to
another suit. We can *signal*. It depends entirely on the *order* in
which we play cards that may be of no importance in themselves.

**Petering.** West opens the king of hearts against four spades.

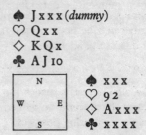

♠ J x x x *(dummy)*
♡ Q x x
♢ K Q x
♣ A J 10

♠ x x x
♡ 9 2
♢ A x x x
♣ x x x x

First, East reads the lead. Yes, it must be the king from A K,
for the queen is on the table and West would not lead an
unsupported king.

East likes the lead, because he has two hearts only and can
ruff the third one.

To encourage West, he plays the *nine* on the king. Then, on
the ace, he will follow with the deuce.

This 'unnatural' sequence – a high card first, a low one next

– is a recognized method of calling on partner to continue. In bridge parlance, the first high card is known as a 'peter'. The low one that follows is called an 'echo'.

Had East been dealt three hearts, instead of two, he would have dropped the deuce on the first trick. That would have shown no interest in the heart suit.

The same position arises in no-trumps.

♠ A K (*dummy*)
♡ Q x x x
♢ K x x x
♣ J x x

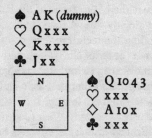

♠ Q 10 4 3
♡ x x x
♢ A 10 x
♣ x x x

West opens a small spade and East plays the *ten* – to encourage partner, because he hopes to see the attack on the spades maintained. If East's hand were:

♠ 10 3    ♡ x x x    ♢ 10 x x x    ♣ A Q 10 x x

he would have no interest in spades. To inform West, he would drop the three. Next time he gained the lead, West might switch to a club – a pleasing prospect.

**Informative Discards.** A variation on this theme occurs when a defender cannot follow to a suit at all. By selecting an informative discard he can often put partner on the right road.

West leads a spade against no-trumps.

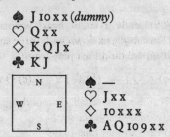

&spades; J 10 x x (*dummy*)
&hearts; Q x x
&diams; K Q J x
&clubs; K J

&spades; —
&hearts; J x x
&diams; 10 x x x
&clubs; A Q 10 9 x x

East throws the *ten* of clubs – to arrest partner's attention. An ostentatious discard of a high card is an obvious peter.

Of course, in this example East's clubs are such that he can afford the ten. But it is a luxury. If the suit is less solid East must try another way of coaxing West to switch to clubs. His lowest heart may achieve the same effect. That would show lack of interest in hearts. Taking a good look at the table, an alert West is unlikely to lead a diamond. And he will reason that, if partner does not like hearts, he must want clubs.

This, broadly speaking, is the rule in signalling:

Encourage by following suit with a high card – an eight or nine, perhaps, when you have the deuce or the four.

Discourage – or show indifference – by following with your lowest.

In discarding, when you cannot follow at all, throw a low card in a suit you don't want led.

Alternatively, but only if you can afford it, peter in a suit to which you hope that partner will switch.

**Epilogue.** *Signalling may appear a little complicated at first. But as you grow used to it, you will find it simple and easy. And that is true of most things in bridge. The game is so logical, that once you grasp its basic principles, you are equipped to solve all those intriguing problems, which make every deal different from the last one – and bridge itself forever fascinating and forever mysterious.*

## Exercises

1. West leads a small heart against three no-trumps by South. Dummy goes down with three small hearts.

What card should East play from:

    (*a*) K Q J    (*b*) K J x    (*c*) Q x x    (*d*) Q J 10

2. West leads a small diamond against one no-trump by South. Dummy plays the ace.

What card should East play?

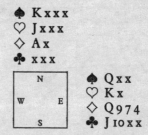

3. Sitting West, you open the knave of diamonds against two no-trumps by South. Declarer wins in his hand with the queen and leads a small spade.

What card do you play?

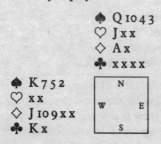

4. Sitting West, you lead the king of hearts against four spades by South. East plays the nine.

What are your chances of breaking the contract?

### Bidding

| N | E | S | W |
|---|---|---|---|
| One diamond | No bid | One spade | No bid |
| Two no-trumps | No bid | Four spades | |

(a)

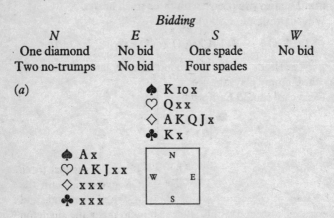

```
                    ♠ K 10 x
                    ♡ Q x x
                    ◇ A K Q J x
                    ♣ K x

        ♠ A x            N
        ♡ A K J x x
        ◇ x x x      W       E
        ♣ x x x
                         S
```

(b) The hands are the same as above, except that you have six hearts and only two clubs. What are your chances this time?

5. Sitting West, you lead the king of diamonds against three no-trumps by South. Partner plays the deuce.

What card do you play next?

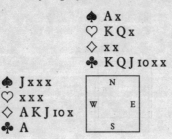

```
                    ♠ A x
                    ♡ K Q x
                    ◇ x x
                    ♣ K Q J 10 x x

        ♠ J x x x        N
        ♡ x x x
        ◇ A K J 10 x  W       E
        ♣ A
                         S
```

6. Sitting West, you lead the queen of spades against three no-trumps by South. Declarer wins in his hand with the king, and leads the king of clubs.

What card do you play?

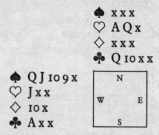

♠ x x x
♡ A Q x
♢ x x x
♣ Q 10 x x

♠ Q J 10 9 x
♡ J x x
♢ 10 x
♣ A x x

7. Sitting West, you open the four of spades against three no-trumps by South. Partner plays the knave and South the ace. Declarer comes to dummy with the ace of diamonds and finesses the queen of clubs, allowing you to make the singleton king.

What card do you play?

*Bidding*

S                         N

One no-trump   Three no-trumps

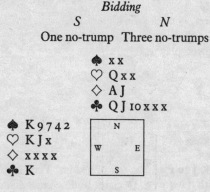

♠ x x
♡ Q x x
♢ A J
♣ Q J 10 x x x

♠ K 9 7 4 2
♡ K J x
♢ x x x x
♣ K

8.                            *Bidding*
              S                N
        One no-trump   Three no-trumps

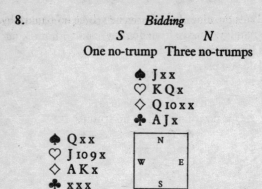

♠ J x x
♡ K Q x
◇ Q 10 x x
♣ A J x

♠ Q x x
♡ J 10 9 x
◇ A K x
♣ x x x

Declarer wins the opening heart lead in his hand, and leads a small diamond.

What card do you play?

9.                            *Bidding*
      N            E           S            W
  One diamond   One spade   Two no-trumps   No bid
  Three no-trumps

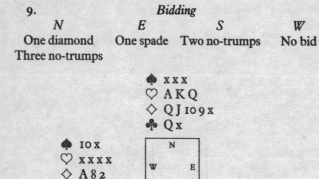

♠ x x x
♡ A K Q
◇ Q J 10 9 x
♣ Q x

♠ 10 x
♡ x x x x
◇ A 8 2
♣ x x x x

Sitting West, you lead the ten of spades. Partner plays the knave and South the queen. Declarer leads a small diamond.
What card do you play?

10. West leads the nine of spades against three no-trumps by South. Declarer plays the ace from dummy.

What card should East play?

### Bidding

| S | N |
|---|---|
| One club | One heart |
| One no-trump | Three no-trumps |

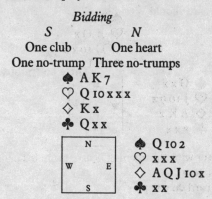

♠ A K 7
♡ Q 10 x x x
♢ K x
♣ Q x x

♠ Q 10 2
♡ x x x
♢ A Q J 10 x
♣ x x

11. West opens the five of clubs against three no-trumps by South.

### Bidding

| S | N |
|---|---|
| One no-trump | Three no-trumps |

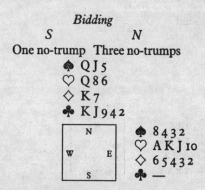

♠ Q J 5
♡ Q 8 6
♢ K 7
♣ K J 9 4 2

♠ 8 4 3 2
♡ A K J 10
♢ 6 5 4 3 2
♣ —

(a) What card should East play?

(b) What card should East play to the second trick, if declarer wins the first one in his hand with the eight, and plays the queen of clubs to West's ace?

12. West leads the king of diamonds against three no-trumps by South. He holds the trick and continues with the queen of diamonds, which also holds.

What card should West play next?

### Bidding

S           N

One no-trump   Three no-trumps

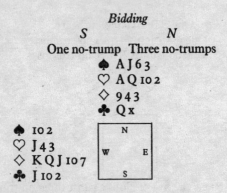

♠ A J 6 3
♡ A Q 10 2
◇ 9 4 3
♣ Q x

♠ 10 2
♡ J 4 3
◇ K Q J 10 7
♣ J 10 2

13. Your partner, West, opens the three of spades against three no-trumps. You win with the ace.

What card should you play?

### Bidding

S           N

One no-trump   Three no-trumps

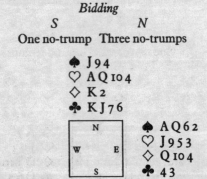

♠ J 9 4
♡ A Q 10 4
◇ K 2
♣ K J 7 6

♠ A Q 6 2
♡ J 9 5 3
◇ Q 10 4
♣ 4 3

14. West opens a small spade against three no-trumps by South. Declarer wins in dummy and leads a diamond to his king, then another diamond, which partner wins with the ace.

What card should East play on the second round of diamonds?

### Bidding

S                           N

One no-trump  Three no-trumps

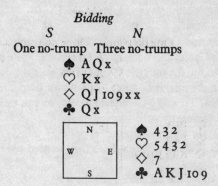

♠ A Q x
♡ K x
♢ Q J 10 9 x x
♣ Q x

♠ 4 3 2
♡ 5 4 3 2
♢ 7
♣ A K J 10 9

15. West opens the three of spades against three no-trumps by South.

What card should you lead, sitting East, after winning the first trick with the ace of spades?

### Bidding

S                           N

One no-trump  Three no-trumps

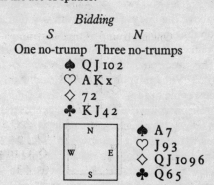

♠ Q J 10 2
♡ A K x
♢ 7 2
♣ K J 4 2

♠ A 7
♡ J 9 3
♢ Q J 10 9 6
♣ Q 6 5

# *Answers to Exercises*

## LESSON I

1. (*a*) 60. Only the tricks for which you contract count towards Game, and nothing else is recorded below the line.

(*b*) 30 for the overtrick – one trick over the contract. It will count in the final reckoning – but not for Game.

(*c*) No. To make Game needs 100, so you need another 40. One spade is only 30.

2. (*a*) In yours, because opponents failed to make their contract. To make four spades they needed ten tricks – 4 plus 6.

(*b*) Above the line. See 1 (*a*) above.

3. (*a*) Opponents score 500 above the line, for you are two down, vulnerable and doubled.

(*b*) You score 180 below the line and 50 above, on your side. You have just fulfilled your contract, and since opponents doubled, it gives you twice 90 – more than enough for Game. The 50 above the line is for the 'insult' – a bonus for bringing home a doubled contract.

(*c*) Again you score 180 below the line, on your side, and 250 above. This time you made a doubled *overtrick* – one more than the contract. Vulnerable, that is worth 200. Non-vulnerable, it would have come to 100.

4. (*a*) Below you write 120 – six times 20. Above you record the Slam bonus, which, non-vulnerable, is 500.

(*b*) Below the line the score is 240. The slam bonus is not affected and remains 500, but you add 50 for the 'insult'.

(*c*) Below the line the score is now 480. Neither the slam points, nor the bonus for the 'insult' are affected.

5. (*a*) 60. See 1 (*a*).

(*b*) 20 for one overtrick. You score nothing for honours as neither you nor your partner held four in *one* hand.

6. (*a*) Nothing. You only score below the line when your side plays the hand, and then only if the contract is fulfilled.

(*b*) 200. You collect a penalty of 100 – one down doubled, non-vulnerable. And you score another 100 for honours. You are entitled to the bonus for honours even though the other side played the hand.

7. (*a*) 20 to you. Their score is 120 – four hearts. Yours is 40 (for two clubs) and 100 above the line, because opponents went one down (seven tricks instead of eight) in their two spade contract.

In adding up the total points no distinction is made between the figures above and below the line.

(*b*) No. The rubber is won by the first side to score *two* games. A grand slam is worth one game only.

8.(*a*) 160 below the line (four times 40) and 50 above for the 'insult'.

(*b*) Still 160 below, but 250 above – 50 for the 'insult' and 200 for one re-doubled overtrick, non-vulnerable. Had you been vulnerable the overtrick would have been worth 400.

(*c*) Again 160 below the line, but 650 above. This time, you made three overtricks – three times 200.

9. Your partner's. The opening lead is always made by the player sitting on the *left* of declarer.

10. Again it is your partner's turn to lead. If clubs were trumps, it would be your lead, but no-trumps were called by the player on your left and he, therefore, is the declarer.

11. 300 to you above the line. The fact that you are vulnerable does not affect the penalty incurred by opponents. Had they been vulnerable, the penalty would have been 500 – regardless of your own vulnerability.

## LESSON II

1. West cannot bid again if South passes. Three successive passes, after a call, close the auction.

2. Four no-trumps. As no-trumps rank higher than spades (or any of the other three suits), a bid in no-trumps can always be made at the *same* level as the previous call.

3. Yes. North can make any bid he likes. Only two successive passes have followed the last call, East's double. Unless a player has already said No Bid, he is always in a position to intervene after a call – any call – by another player.

4. (*a*) In dummy. The lead is always from the hand which won the *previous* trick.

(*b*) It is East's turn to play. All the movements at Bridge are clockwise. Since South is declarer, dummy must be North, and the player on dummy's left is East.

5. No Bid. One club is the lowest bid both in rank and numbers. To make it possible, the other three players at the table must have passed.

6. South can re-double, but not East. No player can double or re-double a contract which has already been doubled or re-doubled by his partner, any more than he can double his own contract. Opponents, of course, can do as they like.

7. (*a*) West. The second pack is always shuffled by the dealer's partner.

(*b*) South. As always, the movement is to the left – clockwise.

8. No further bidding is possible by any player. Since no one can hold more (or less) than thirteen cards, there is no way of making – or contracting to make – more than thirteen tricks. As no-trumps is the highest denomination, there can be no higher contract than seven no-trumps. The double and the

redouble exhaust the only two other bids available.

9. Dummy goes down immediately *after* the opening lead.

10. No. Dummy can only point out irregularities. Mistakes – no matter how obvious or how expensive – do not come under that heading.

The only exception to this rule is dummy's right to warn partner that he is *about to play* from the wrong hand.

## LESSON III

1. 13: Eleven in high card points and two more for the long spades – two cards in excess of four.

2. 18: With a 4–3–3–3 pattern there can be no distributional values.

3. 13: Ten high card points and one each for the fifth, sixth and seventh spade.

4. One club. With no guard at all in hearts, this is better than one no-trump. If partner responds a diamond or a heart, the rebid is one spade – still at the one level, you will note. If you *open* one spade, you may find yourself in trouble for a rebid – especially if responder calls two hearts.

5. No bid. The hand is worth 12 points only and there is no distributional value at all.

6. One spade. With touching suits of equal length, *always* bid the higher ranking suit first. On the next round you can bid hearts.

7. One no-trump. The hand is balanced and there is an honour in every suit. The knave of spades is not a certain guard, of course, but it helps. Partner, too, may have an honour.

8. One heart. Always bid the *longest* suit first, regardless of high cards.

9. (*a*) One spade. As partner has already passed, you need

not worry about a rebid. His hand is *limited* to 12 points at the outside and there is, therefore, little danger of missing a game. Whatever he responds, you intend to pass.

(*b*) One club. With 17 points you are too good for one no-trump, and it is better to stretch the quality of the suit – especially clubs – than to mislead partner about your strength. With 9–10 points he will pass one no-trump and a likely game will be missed.

(*c*) One diamond. You must be prepared for a response in hearts. Then you can show your spades without *raising the level*. If you open one spade and partner calls two hearts, you will have to suppress the diamonds altogether or call them at the level of three.

Always think ahead – and envisage the most awkward response from partner.

10. (*a*) One heart. Over two clubs from partner – the least welcome response – you rebid two diamonds.

(*b*) One diamond. This time, your rebid – over two clubs – will be two diamonds. A five-card suit is always rebiddable.

## LESSON IV

1. Three no-trumps. You have enough for Game with 13 points – 11 in high cards and 2 more for the long clubs. But you are far more likely to make nine tricks in no-trumps than eleven in clubs.

A solid suit (no losers) is especially valuable in no-trumps. In this case, it guarantees six tricks as soon as partner takes the lead.

2. Two no-trumps. If partner has a minimum, the combined total is only 24. So let him decide whether or not to bid the Game.

3. Two hearts. It is a *weakness takeout* and the opener must

not bid again. Clearly, the hand will yield more tricks in hearts than in no-trumps.

4. Three spades. If the opener has three spades, he will call four. If he has a doubleton, three no-trumps will probably turn out to be the best contract. You must be in Game, of course, and partner cannot pass a *forcing* bid.

5. Two no-trumps. With 11 points, all suits guarded, a balanced hand and no four-card major, it is the ideal hand – in shape and strength – for a two no-trump response. Partner can pass if he has a minimum.

6. One heart. This time, it costs nothing to show a major. Partner may also have four hearts, and if he has, that should be the best contract. The weakness in diamonds makes a bid of two no-trumps inadvisable.

7. Three clubs. You have no other suit to show, and without a guard in hearts it would be unwise to call no-trumps.

If the opener has a minimum, he will pass three clubs.

8. Two no-trumps. Showing a club fit is not very constructive on this hand. With a guard in every suit it is best to tell partner of your strength and shape, allowing him to call the Game if he has anything over a minimum.

9. Four hearts. Having found a fit in one major, no purpose would be served in showing the other.

10. Two hearts. The opener will know that you have a weak hand, but that you quite like his hearts. Unless he is very strong, he will pass and you will probably find yourselves in your best contract.

11. One heart. It is more constructive to show a major than a minor, and the hand is not good enough to respond at the two level.

12. One heart. Again, it is more constructive to show a major than to confirm the fit in diamonds. If partner bids two diamonds – or two hearts – you pass. If his rebid is in another suit, you put him back to diamonds.

13. Three diamonds. It is the natural bid, and by inference denies a biddable four-card major. Should partner rebid three no-trumps, you pass. You *don't* take him back to diamonds on the grounds that you have nothing in hearts or spades. Leave that to him.

14. Four spades. Having found a fit in one of the majors, you bid the full value of your hand.

15. Three no-trumps. You have a very good hand and four spades will probably be a make, too. But if partner has four spades only, three no-trumps will be the safer contract. With a completely balanced hand – not even a doubleton – it is best to look for game in no-trumps.


# LESSON V

1. Two Hearts. That shows a minimum opening, and a rebiddable suit.

2. Two no-trumps. That tells partner everything (17–18 points and a balanced hand) except the length in hearts. If partner has heart support – K x x or even J x x – he can still show it by calling three hearts.

3. Two spades. With four cards in a major bid by partner, *always* raise him at once unless you are too good for a Game raise. As your hand has minimum values, you are worth two spades only.

Have no regrets about those good-looking hearts. They will make just as many tricks with spades as trumps, as if they were trumps themselves.

4. Two clubs. That gives partner the widest range of bids. He can show *preference* between hearts and clubs, and he can show diamonds at the two level, if he has a spade-diamond two suiter. With a singleton, the rebid of one no-trump is not advisable.

5. Four hearts. With a 19 count (allowing 2 for the long hearts) there is no alternative. The hand should be rebid to Game, and three hearts can be passed.

6. Three diamonds. A slam may be on and you are therefore too good to call four spades. The only way to fire responder's imagination is to FORCE on the second round – to jump in a new suit. Whatever action he takes – and he cannot pass a force – you will call spades on the next round.

7. Three clubs. That is a *sign off*, showing length in your suit, but insufficient values for three no-trumps. The opener must pass. He has made a *limited* bid, announcing 16–17 points. You know his hand, while he does not know yours. Therefore, he must respect your decision about the final contract.

Of course, if your hand were even slightly better, you would bid three no-trumps.

8. Three no-trumps. Partner's rebid shows that he has something in every suit, so you need not be deterred by the fact that all your strength is in clubs.

Three clubs, as in 7 above, would be a Sign Off. You are too good for that. On the other hand, you cannot expect to collect eleven tricks for a Game in clubs.

9. Four hearts. Partner has shown a very strong hand, 19–20 points, but hearts look better than no-trumps. After all, something might go wrong with the spades. The four heart bid shows no extra strength whatever – only length.

10. No bid. There is no purpose in rebidding a five-card suit at the four level.

11. Six diamonds. Partner has shown 19–20 points, so you have between you more than the slam quota of 34. In diamonds, the hand may play better than in no-trumps, for declarer may be able to ruff a spade.

12. Two spades. With the same length in both his suits, put partner back to the first one. He *may* well have more spades than hearts.

13. **Three spades.** Again you prefer spades, but you are *too good* for simple preference. Without the king of hearts, two spades would be enough.

14. **Two no-trumps.** You have just the right values, 11 points and something in every suit. With only a doubleton in each of partner's suits, no-trumps is more constructive than a preference bid.

15. (*a*) **No bid.** Partner's response is encouraging, but not forcing, and with a minimum opening, you have nothing more to say.

(*b*) **Three spades.** Partner's response is *unconditionally* forcing as he has not yet passed. By re-bidding spades you show a five- (or six-) card suit, but no additional strength.

(*c*) **Three spades.** Partner's force in clubs shows a big hand, but not necessarily a good or long suit. If he calls clubs again, raise him. Meanwhile let him know that you have at least five spades.

16. **No bid.** A *double* jump shows a weak hand and a long suit. With diamonds or clubs as trumps you may be unable to make a single trick in partner's hand.

17. **One diamond.** You are far too strong for an opening three diamonds, which partner would pass on quite a good hand.

18. **Three hearts.** The purpose is to raise a barrage against opponents – to make it difficult for them to exchange information. If partner has nothing, you will go three down. But it will be worth it as opponents must have a certain game, and quite likely, a slam.

19. **No bid.** Compare this hand with the last one. You will see at a glance that the two hands together do not add up to a game, and there is no reason why partner should have more than is shown in Question 18.

20. **Three hearts.** Look up Question 16. This could easily be the hand opposite. Note that opponents can probably make

four spades. The reason for the double jump in hearts is to shut them out, if possible.

## LESSON VI

1. Two no-trumps. You have all the qualifications for that bid – every suit guarded and a count of 21.

2. Two hearts. Not quite a two-club bid, since you cannot make Game on your own. But you have about eight *playing* tricks and a good long suit.

3. Two clubs. If responder bids two diamonds – as is only to be expected – you call two no-trumps, showing near Game values and a balanced hand.

4. Two diamonds. Of course, opposite a Game Demand bid you have an excellent hand. But you lack the *high card* values– an ace and a king – for a *positive* response. You will have to show how good you are later in the auction, but not on the first round.

5. Two no-trumps. This time, you have the requirements for a positive response. No-trumps shows a balanced hand, and therefore promises a *fit* in whatever may be partner's suit.

6. Four spades. This shows good trump support, some strength but no controls.

7. Three spades. A single raise suggests an ace and it is always advisable to support partner's suit at the first opportunity. Expecting a 6-card suit opposite, your trump support is more than adequate.

8. Two no-trumps. You have enough to keep the bidding open. On ACOL it is compulsory for one round.

9. Three no-trumps. As in 8, a balanced hand, but a good deal *more* than you might have.

10. Two no-trumps. The *conventional* response on nothing.

You must not drop the bidding till Game level.

11. Three no-trumps. See 9 above. You have the shape for no-trumps, but two would be a denial and you are too good for that.

12. Five diamonds, showing *one* ace.

13. Five spades, showing *three* aces.

14. No bid. The combined hands should add up to 30–31 points, which is not enough for a slam. Partner may well have both the missing aces, but that will not enable you to make twelve tricks. There is, therefore, no occasion to use the Blackwood convention.

15. Four no-trumps. You want to be in a slam, but it is just possible that two aces may be missing. Partner could have: ♠Axxxx ♡QJx ◇QJx ♣Kx. To make certain, ask for aces. Use Blackwood to guard against bad slams – not to get into good ones.

16. No bid. Blackwood operates only *after* a suit has been agreed. When only no-trumps have been called, the convention does not apply. Partner is making a natural – quantitative – bid, asking you to bid a slam, if you have anything to spare. You have not, so you pass.

17. Six no-trumps. This time you have a full-blooded two no-trumps opening and accept the invitation.

18. Four hearts. Opposite a three bid you cannot envisage a slam. Locating an ace in partner's hand would not help, and he can hardly have two aces. You should not think of Blackwood on this hand.

19. Four no-trumps. If partner has an ace, you want to be in six. This is the time for Blackwood. Of course, if the response is five clubs (no ace) you call five hearts.

20. Six hearts. There is no point in showing the spades in which partner may well have a void. In any case, the search for a trump suit is over, since you can be fairly certain of ten hearts between the two hands.

A grand slam is out of the question. Partner is not likely to have both the king of hearts and the ace of diamonds.

## LESSON VII

1. Double. You have a very fair hand, but no worthwhile suit of your own. Double – *informatively*, of course – to find out about partner's hand.

2. No bid. You must not double since you cannot stand a response in spades. Without a guard in that suit it would also be unwise to call one no-trump. When most of your strength is in a suit bid by opponents, it is generally best to pass.

3. *Two* spades. There is no point in doubling, for with a good, long suit of your own you do not really want to know about partner's. Hearing a jump overcall, he will raise you on very little – which is just what you want him to do.

4. One spade. It is about a minimum, but you are calling at the one level only. And it is more important to show spades than any other suit, for you can outbid opponents at the same level. Note the difference in strength between this example and the last. Hence the jump overcall on 3.

5. Three spades. This, of course, is a *pre-emptive* bid, intended to crowd the opponents. A double jump does *not* show a strong hand, only a long suit, six or seven playing tricks and little or no defence.

6. Three diamonds. Note that this is a single – not a double – jump, and therefore, shows a strong hand, as well as a long suit. Partner will try for game – perhaps in three no-trumps – on very little.

7. Double. Your hand is worth at least five tricks in defence, but may be of little use except in spades. A penalty is pretty certain. Anything else is problematical. A double of a low level contract generally suggests shortage in partner's suit. You are,

therefore, conveying a perfect picture of your hand.

Note that since partner has made a positive bid – not a pass – your double is *not* informatory.

8. Two no-trumps. That is the natural bid with two probable stoppers in spades, a count of 11 and a balanced hand.

9. One no-trump. The same type of hand as above, but not quite so good.

10. Four hearts. There can be no question of doubling one spade – firstly, because your spades are bad; secondly because you are pretty certain to make four hearts, maybe even six: and lastly because you want to shut out opponents who may be able to find a cheap sacrifice in diamonds.

11. No bid. To double one spade would be thoughtless, and would lead partner to expect a better hand. He might double opponents in some other contract, and this would not suit you at all.

12. Two diamonds. You have enough to call three no-trumps, but with one guard only in spades it is better to see first if partner can rebid his hearts. If he does, give him four.

Note that partner cannot drop the bidding. As you have not passed, your bid in a new suit is forcing.

13. Two hearts. You are too good to call one heart, which you would have had to do on the same hand without the ace or king of diamonds.

14. No bid. With such good clubs you leave the double in, expecting a useful penalty. Partner clearly has something in the other three suits, but you have no fit for them and no entry to the solid-looking clubs. That rules out no-trumps – the only alternative to passing.

15. One no-trump. This is more constructive than one diamond, which is the only other possibility.

16. Four spades. Partner's double guarantees some support for spades and promises enough all-round strength to warrant a game contract. With a six-card major, bid the full value of your hand.

Note that partner could pass *two* spades. A jump in response to a double is encouraging, but not forcing.

17. Three no-trumps. There is no point at all in showing the diamonds. Partner is unlikely to have a club guard and cannot, therefore, call no-trumps himself. Yet that is the obvious contract, and opposite an informatory double, you have quite enough for game.

18. One spade. Show your *longest* suit – particularly when it is a major. Partner must be prepared for a response in spades, so you need not be unduly apprehensive about the trump suit.

19. No bid. You may easily go three down in five diamonds – far too much in view of the unequal vulnerability, and you certainly must not think of doubling four spades, for your hand is worth no more than two tricks in defence – may be even, one only. The diamonds may not make a trick at all and the queen of spades is on the *wrong* side – under the spade bid.

20. Double. This is a much better defensive hand than the last, because your suits are short and none of your cards are badly placed – in finessible positions. The ace of diamonds is worth more than the ace, king and queen in the last hand, for there is not the same risk that one of the defenders will have a void.

# LESSON VIII

1. A diamond. You can see six certain winners. You need one more for your contract, and the correct play is to attack the suit in which you and dummy, between you, hold the *most* cards.

Opponents have only five diamonds. If they are divided 3–2, it will take three rounds to set up a diamond.

Note that as you play the suit, opponents' honours will crash. The knave and the ten may fall *together* on the first trick, and the king and queen on the second.

2. A spade. You can see seven winners and need, therefore, one more. Two rounds of spades will drive out the ace and king, setting up a spade honour in dummy.

3. The ten. South can see nine tricks for his contract, so long as he can set up dummy's clubs. But there is a danger that East or West started with five spades and will take four tricks in that suit, in addition to the ace of clubs.

If five spades and the ace of clubs are in the same hand, there is no hope. But if they are *divided*, South gains by holding up his king till the *third* round. Then the defender with the ace of clubs may have no more spades left to give his partner the lead.

The *hold up* may kill the vital entry to the hand with the five spades.

4. The ace. South has nine 'top' – ready-made – tricks. He is not interested in the spade suit at all. But if he holds up his ace, leaving East on play, a real danger may arise. East may switch to *hearts* in which suit declarer has no certain guard.

5. A small spade from both hands. South needs four spade tricks for his contract and must hope for the likely 3–2 split of the spades against him. Dummy's only entry – the king of spades – must not be used *before* the x's have been set up. Since one of the defenders must have three spades, the suit will not be established till the third round.

6. A small club. Declarer can make nine tricks – two spades, four hearts, two diamonds, and a club – easily enough. There is one danger. If either defender has five clubs, five tricks may be lost *first*. Should the same defender have five (or more) clubs and the ace of spades, the contract is doomed. But if the outstanding clubs break 5–2, the defender with the ace of spades may be the one who is short in clubs. And if that is the case, he will not have a club to return – so long as *two* rounds of clubs are played before declarer touches spades.

Note that it will not matter if the defender with the ace of spades has three clubs. The suit will then break 4–3 – not 5–2, and that will mean that the defence will not have enough club tricks to beat the contract.

7. A small diamond. Declarer needs five tricks in diamonds for his contract and the suit cannot break better than 3–2. It will, therefore, require three rounds to clear the suit – to exhaust the defender with three diamonds. By giving up the first trick – instead of the second or the third – declarer ensures that the lead will be in dummy when the suit has been established.

The vital link with dummy is declarer's doubleton diamond and he must keep one for the *third*, decisive round. If he does not, he can still set up the long diamonds. But he will have no means of getting at them, for dummy has no entry.

8. The knave of spades. At first sight, it looks as if you should lead a heart to knock out dummy's entry to the clubs. But it is not necessary. As soon as you have knocked out declarer's second stopper in spades, you have set up five tricks – enough to break the contract.

Always keep your eye on the target – the number of tricks needed to set the contract.

9. The king of diamonds. Partner's spades can wait. The first consideration is to prevent declarer from developing four club tricks. Dummy's ace of diamonds is the vital entry and must be removed at all cost.

Note that you must play the king, not a small one, for declarer may have the knave of diamonds, and if he can win the trick in his hand, the entry to the table will remain.

10. Dummy's knave and the *ace* from the closed hand. Declarer needs an entry to the clubs and must preserve the king of spades. Unless he 'gets rid' of the ace on the first round, it will stand in the way of the king – the vital entry to the Table.

# LESSON IX

1. (a) Any club from North and the *ace* from South.

  (b) The ten of hearts from South and an x from dummy.

The contract depends on the heart finesse and declarer must, therefore, lead from his hand, hoping that West has the king.

If he leads a small heart, not the ten, he will find himself in dummy, even if the king is right. That won't do, because the finesse must be *repeated*, in case West has K x x. Only the ten will allow South to retain the lead in his own hand – unless, of course, West covers with the king.

2. (a) Any diamond from North and the *ace* from South.

  (b) A small heart from South and the *ten* from dummy.

Declarer has eleven tricks on top, and the twelfth must come from the heart suit. South should give himself all the chances by taking finesses in hearts. If East takes the ten of hearts with the knave, South can still finesse against the king.

To lead through West *twice*, South needs two entries in his own hand and should, therefore, win the first trick with the ace of diamonds. The second entry will be the ace of spades.

3. Yes. South probably has the ace and queen of the suit, but West may have 10 x x. By covering the knave with the king, East may promote partner's ten. If South has A Q 10, nothing is lost by covering.

4. The king. If East has the ace, there is nothing to be done about it, but if West has it, the king will win.

The point to bear in mind is that East won't play his ace – if he has it – on the small heart. If South goes up with dummy's king, he *may* succeed. If he does not, he is doomed – whichever defender has the ace.

5. A small one. This time, South can make absolutely certain of his contract. If East plays any card lower than the

knave, South wins and reels off nine top tricks. If East goes up with the ace or king, declarer can still stop the suit.

The same play is correct if dummy's holding is K x instead of Q x.

6. No. With a singleton in dummy, the finesse cannot be repeated. Therefore, East's king can never be caught. Promoting a ten or nine in West's hand is a possibility. Conserving the king is a certainty.

If dummy had one more spade and East one less, then it would be proper to cover.

7. No. It is rarely correct to cover the first of *touching* honours. If the knave holds and declarer leads dummy's ten, then West covers.

8. Yes. This is the exception to the principle set out in Question 7, above. Work it out. If East plays the ten on the queen, declarer cannot fail to make three tricks. The ace will kill the king on the next round, and the nine will then be master. If East goes up with the king, declarer must still find the ten. Should he guess wrongly, he will be kept to two tricks – instead of three.

9. No. On the bidding, partner can have at most one spade – probably none at all. Covering the queen cannot, therefore, *promote* anything. Remember that the one reason for covering honours is to promote lesser honours – or nines and eights. When there can be nothing to promote, play low.

10. (*a*) The knave. If West has led from the queen, the knave will hold. If East has the queen, he will not waste it on dummy's x, but will probably finesse against dummy. Playing the knave can win, but is unlikely to lose.

(*b*) No. This time, declarer can make certain of two tricks by playing low. Unless East goes up with an honour, the ten will take the first trick. If East plays the king or queen, declarer wins, and the 10 x in his hand opposite the knave in dummy must yield another trick.

# LESSON X

1. The queen of spades. Two more spades follow, dummy's heart loser being discarded on the third spade. Now South can ruff both his heart losers in dummy.

The grand slam is made with: five trumps; three spades; two clubs; the ace of hearts; and two heart ruffs on the table.

2. (*a*) Dummy.

(*b*) A diamond. It is always correct to lead a small card towards the king – or K Q – in case the ace is under the king.

Here South has another reason as well. He may want to ruff *two* diamonds. If he wins the first heart in his hand, he will be short of an entry, later, to ruff the second diamond.

South's danger is that the defence will be able to draw three trumps from dummy – first ace and another, and then a third trump. So he must be careful to prevent the defence coming in twice before he has finished ruffing diamonds.

3. (*a*) His own hand.

(*b*) A spade. Declarer needs all his three entries on the table to set up the spades.

He cashes the ace of spades, crosses to dummy with the ace of hearts and ruffs a spade; goes over with the ace of diamonds and ruffs again. Now he draws trumps and gets back to dummy with the ace of clubs.

He makes: six trump tricks; four spades; and two aces.

4. (*a*) His own hand.

(*b*) A small club and the queen. South must set up the clubs. If the finesse against the king succeeds, he plays the ace and ruffs a third club in his hand – with an honour, if East follows. Then he draws trumps, ending in dummy. If the finesse fails, South can still set up the club suit – so long as he is careful to leave the king of trumps in dummy as an entry.

5. A diamond. West can see that it is no use forcing declarer, since he has trumps 'to burn'. Two more tricks are needed to break the contract and the only hope is that East has the ace of diamonds. A diamond ruff will then be the setting trick.

6. A diamond. South must not allow himself to be forced, because then he would be afraid to draw trumps. If East or West has four, trump control will pass to the defence. The second or third club will be ruffed and South will have no trump left to stop the hearts. But if he refuses to ruff the second heart, South need not worry. A third heart can be ruffed on the table – without shortening his own trump holding.

7. A diamond ruff in dummy will be the tenth trick. Declarer plays three rounds of hearts, discarding a diamond from the table. Then the ace and another diamond. Now the stage is set for a diamond ruff. Note that declarer should ruff with the *king* – in case East can over-ruff. Therefore, he must win the first trick in his hand – not in dummy.

8. On a cross-ruff, making his trumps separately. Three spades are ruffed in dummy and three diamonds in the closed hand. Trumps are not touched at all.

9. East should lead a small trump. It is clear that declarer hopes to ruff diamonds in dummy, and it is in the interests of the defence to reduce dummy's ruffing value to a minimum.

10. A heart. The best defence here is to set up a heart trick for partner, and later, to force declarer. There is no point in leading a trump, for declarer can ruff nothing in dummy.

Force declarer when you have length in trumps; lead trumps when dummy has ruffing value.

## LESSON XI

1. The knave of clubs. Attack from length, and in doing so, lead the top of the sequence.

2. The king of diamonds. Although North bid the suit, your sequence is so solid that the lead can hardly help declarer.

3. The top of the three little clubs. The spades would provide the obvious lead – if South had not bid them. Since he has, partner is unlikely to hold anything in the suit and the lead into declarer's tenace would cost a trick.

The club is the best of a bad job and 'top of nothing' is the correct lead.

4. The queen of hearts. You hope to force declarer to win the first trick, so that when partner gains the lead he should have a heart left to put you in. If partner has no entry, there is no hope anyway.

5. The singleton heart. You need four tricks to beat the contract and partner is unlikely to produce them on his own. But if he has the ace of hearts, you can get a ruff – and maybe two ruffs, if you find partner with a second entry.

6. The ace of diamonds. In suit contracts you should not lead a small card away from an ace.

7. The lowest diamond. From a three-card combination, headed by a high honour, the lowest x is the right opening.

8. The knave of spades. That is unlikely to cost a trick, whatever the distribution. If the contract were three no-trumps, a diamond would be correct. When partner got in, he would play another diamond – through declarer's king, perhaps – and four tricks might be made in that suit by West to break the contract.

In six, if East can get in at all, the ace of diamonds by itself will break the contract. But defending against a slam, one does not expect partner to have an entry, when holding an ace oneself.

A diamond opening is bad, because it is almost certain to present declarer with a trick. There is a good chance that declarer, with 11 tricks only, will try to make his twelfth trick by playing a diamond himself, and if the king is in the South hand, you will make two tricks.

9. The singleton heart. This time, partner may well have the ace of hearts or a trump entry. If East gains the lead before West's trumps are drawn, he will give his partner a heart ruff.

10. Queen of spades. Though the diamonds are longer, you have no likely entry, even should you succeed in establishing the suit. Besides, there is the danger of leading into the A Q or A Q 10.

Lead from a solid sequence, whenever possible.

11. King of spades. Do not touch the top diamonds. Preserve them as entries for the spades. Note that you do not lead the fourth highest spade. That is because you have a near-sequence.

12. The six of hearts – the fourth highest. It is a broken suit, but you have length and a certain entry. If partner can help at all, you may be able to do a lot of damage. You must hope, of course, that partner has as much as the J x and that he will return the suit *before* your ace of spades is driven out.

13. The knave of diamonds. You have nothing to set up in spades and it is best to wait for the lead in that suit to come to you.

14. Queen of diamonds. With four trumps it is rarely wise to lead a singleton. You hope to make two trump tricks anyway. The best line of attack is to set up the diamonds, and perhaps, to force declarer.

15. A trump. You do not want to lead away from your unsupported honours in the other suits, and the bidding indicates that declarer will find ruffing value in dummy. A

trump – followed by a second trump later, perhaps – will reduce this ruffing value.

# LESSON XII

1. (*a*) The knave – the lowest of touching honours. This is a general rule.

(*b*) The king. Observe the rule: third man plays high. This applies *unless* there is an honour in dummy against which East can finesse. Since dummy has no honour, you can only lose by playing the knave. Work it out. West may have led from the A 10xxx, and in that case, declarer has Qx.

Finesse against dummy, but never against partner.

(*c*) The queen. When dummy has no high card in the suit opened by partner, play your highest. This will drive out declarer's ace or king and help partner to set up his suit.

(*d*) The ten. As in (*a*) play the lowest of touching honours. All three cards are equal, but the lowest is the most informative to partner.

2. The nine. This is a 'peter' – an encouraging card, telling partner that you like diamonds.

3. A small spade. The king can wait. Perhaps, declarer will play dummy's ten, allowing East to make the knave.

There is another reason for not parting with the king. East may have the ace – though not the knave. If so, West wants to preserve his spade entry, hoping that East will return a diamond and help to clear the suit before the entries to it – the two black kings – are driven out.

4. (*a*) It is a certainty. East's nine is an obvious 'peter'. He can only want a heart continuation for one reason – because he has a doubleton and will ruff on the third round. The ace of trumps will be the fourth trick.

Note that if East had three hearts, the nine could not be his lowest. That is why it 'must' be a signal.

(b) Very poor indeed. If East has two hearts, so has declarer, who will be able to over-ruff. On the bidding, South must have the ace of clubs. So your only chance is that partner's nine of hearts is not a 'peter', but a singleton. Play the king and hope for the best.

5. The ace of diamonds. Certainly, partner's deuce is discouraging – but that does not surprise you in the least. Let declarer make his queen. Since you hold the all-important ace of clubs, you can break the contract *without* help from partner. By setting up your diamonds you can make certain of five tricks – four diamonds and the ace of clubs. No need to bother about anything else.

6. A small club. You must strive, at all cost, to retain the ace of clubs as the only likely entry to the spades. Maybe partner has the knave of clubs and will be able to take the next trick and return a spade. If declarer has the knave of clubs, you lose nothing. Your ace will still make a trick – a few seconds later.

7. A small spade. It is vital to realize that partner has the queen of spades. If declarer had it, he would not have played the ace on the first trick.

Should you play the king first, then a small one to partner's queen, he may not have another spade to return. Your spades will be set up – but declarer will make nine tricks before you can get them.

8. The small one. Do not be in a hurry to part with your tops. Maybe declarer is missing the knave and will finesse the ten. Give him a chance to go wrong.

9. The ace. This time, there is a hurry – to preserve partner's king of diamonds, if he has it, as an entry to the spades. If declarer has the king of diamonds himself, your play can make no difference.

The moral is: when partner has a suit to establish, nurse his entries.

10. The deuce. East wants urgently a switch to diamonds, not a spade continuation. Therefore, he plays his most discouraging card.

Note that partner's lead – the nine – suggests 'top of nothing', not a long suit.

11. (a) Two of spades
   (b) Two of diamonds } or vice versa.

East wants his partner to switch to hearts, but cannot afford to part with a high heart since he needs all four to break the contract. By telling West that he does not want spades or diamonds, he leaves him to draw the obvious inference.

12. Knave of clubs. West must abandon his good-looking diamonds, because he has no entry. A club switch looks like being the best chance to embarrass declarer.

13. The deuce. When you have four or more cards in partner's suit, return the fourth highest.

Work out the position. Declarer probably has the king. If you return the queen, he will make two tricks – the king and the knave. But the lead suggests four spades with partner and that means a doubleton in South's hand. The king will, therefore, drop on the deuce; the queen will kill dummy's knave next time.

14. The ace (or king) of clubs. You want urgently a club switch and you can afford to 'peter' demonstratively, because you can make enough tricks to beat the contract. Compare this example with 11.

If you had four clubs only, instead of five, you would throw the deuce of hearts – having played the deuce of spades on the first trick.

15. The queen of diamonds. A spade back can do no good, for dummy can stop the suit twice. Try to set up the diamonds and hope that the queen of clubs will be your entry.

It is generally the best policy to return partner's suit, but it is not an iron rule. Treat every case on its merits.